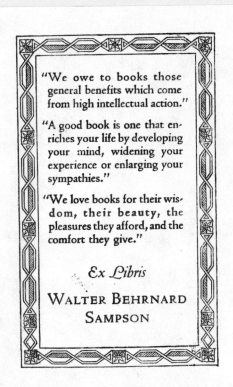

"We owe to books those general benefits which come from high intellectual action."

"A good book is one that enriches your life by developing your mind, widening your experience or enlarging your sympathies."

"We love books for their wisdom, their beauty, the pleasures they afford, and the comfort they give."

Ex Libris

WALTER BEHRNARD
SAMPSON

2174

THE YANKEE OF THE YARDS

GUSTAVUS FRANKLIN SWIFT ABOUT 1902.   A PASS
CARD FOR VISITORS ABOUT THAT TIME.

THE YANKEE OF THE YARDS

THE BIOGRAPHY OF
GUSTAVUS FRANKLIN SWIFT

By
LOUIS F. SWIFT
IN COLLABORATION WITH
ARTHUR VAN VLISSINGEN, JR.

♦

CHICAGO & NEW YORK
A. W. SHAW COMPANY
LONDON, A. W. SHAW AND COMPANY, LIMITED
1927

COPYRIGHT, 1927, BY A. W. SHAW COMPANY
PRINTED IN THE UNITED STATES OF AMERICA

FOREWORD

SHEER accident has swept many men to that slight height above their fellows which the world calls fame or attainment or success. At their sides stand others who reached the same place by ceaseless work and native shrewdness.

For this reason the life stories of most outstanding men lack interest except to the unimaginative who worship success for its own sake. Accidents which turn out well make dull tales, toiling plodders make still duller.

Rare indeed is the man who attains preeminence with the steady, irresistible thrust—who leaves in those who started with him a sense that his progress was inevitable, that one could no more have stopped him than an Alpine glacier or a Sierra cascade. Such a man, to be sure, combines ability and gluttony for work. But to these sober, uninteresting virtues their owner has the good fortune to add being born at a time and place which make his every stroke count for two or ten or ten thousand times the strokes of men who came before or will come after. Every circumstance from his birth to his grave seems calculated to give him a lead over his fellows. Every apparent misfortune turns out to be his lucky chance.

So it was with the first Vanderbilt. Rockefeller and Ford are subsequent examples in the field of

American industry. And had young Bonaparte been born fifteen years after he was, he would have been a child instead of a lieutenant when France burst into fire. For all his military genius and burning ambition he would probably have served his country as a pompous little colonel of the Guards, while the world went ways far different from those history records.

What created of a corporal an emperor, of these other men the chief commercial figures of their times? For want of a better name we call it destiny, that motive power which makes life interesting—and which makes interesting lives. For it smacks of destiny when force and industry and shrewdness are found in conjunction, with all the auspices favorable to their most effective use.

Destiny it was which presided at the birth of a boy in a Cape Cod village ninety-odd years ago. He was not to change the world's maps, nor make military history. Instead, he was the human instrument by which destiny transformed the world's sources and supplies of an essential class of foodstuffs. From a start which at first glance seems inauspicious, he built a knowledge and an ability that were to serve him well when circumstances called them into full play.

A younger son of a large family on a sandy, unfertile farm in the dreadful '40s, he did not have much of a chance; yet—his elder brothers were butchers and from them he learned the ins and outs of the trade on which he built. New England was a long way from the plains which sent it cattle; still—here a trade current was first felt which lent its strength to the young butcher's brawny blows on Fortune's door. Chicago in the '70s was a sprawling city with little to recommend it to his energies except a plentiful supply of cattle from the western plains. The Yankee left its "Yards" the undisputed meat-packing center of the hungry world.

That he accomplished so much may be surprising, but it is not necessarily of great interest. That he gained great wealth in the process is neither surprising nor worth more than passing comment. That he worked hard, was honest, practiced the homely copybook virtues is neither here nor there.

The salty, spicy fact is that destiny swept him on to accomplishment extraordinary in any one man's career, that his abilities and the world's changing needs came together to produce a career as exceptional as it is interesting. His battles and his victories were in the field of business. It is this, and not the material success he attained, which makes the chronicle of his life a chronicle of commerce.

For destiny, that spinner of men's threads of life, decreed that business should be his skein. . . . . .

CONTENTS

XI

ILLUSTRATIONS

THE YANKEE OF THE YARDS

CHAPTER I

"A DOLLAR WASTED. . . . "

ANYONE whose work kept him on the bank of Chicago's old "Bubbly Creek back of the Yards" was not to be envied his job in the 1880s and '90s. The marvel was that he would hold the job. For where today a boulevard is building astride a huge tiled channel, thirty years ago there ran a malodorous open sewer.

In his turn the workman had something to marvel at: the regularity with which another man visited this unattractive locality. The frequent visitor was a tall bearded man above middle age. He invariably wore a dark suit with a tail coat, and usually a stiff hat. His stoop suggested desk work. His bearing suggested authority. To the knees he had the appearance of a business proprietor fresh from his private office.

At the knees his appearance shifted abruptly. The tailored trousers disappeared into a plebeian pair of top-boots. The cowhide bore unmistakable traces of wear outside the counting room. Plainly the visitor was not one who devoted his time exclusively to papers and meetings and that nebulous science called management.

This man was my father, Gustavus Franklin Swift.

3

Even after Swift & Company was well established on a large scale, he would frequently visit the bank of Bubbly Creek. He had, in fact, gone to the trouble of finding out where the company's sewer emptied into Old Bubbly; this point was his invariable objective.

It was not a pleasant place to visit. In those days sewage disposal was more direct than scientific. One might have pardoned the head of a large business for avoiding it altogether.

But down to Bubbly Creek father would go, and scrutinize the sewer outlet for a few minutes every once in a while. He was on the lookout for waste. If he saw any fat coming out, that evidenced waste in the packing house. Briskly he would head for the superintendent's office. And before the episode was closed, someone would smart.

His long suit was keeping expenses down. Next in his interest, perhaps, came developing by-products—which is another form of the same thing. Low expenses and maximum return from every pound of the live animal are what made G. F. Swift a leader in the new industry of which he was a founder. For even at the start of his career as a Chicago packer, when margins were not narrowed down as they have been since, he recognized that waste and accomplishment are incompatible. A dollar wasted is gone forever—with no one the better off for its going.

It was his constant seeking after ways to save—a frugality engendered and inbred by ancestors who for two hundred and fifty years had fought a none too equal battle with the miserly sands of Cape Cod— which led the Yankee from Massachusetts and out to the stockyards of Chicago. It was his never-failing creed of economy which built under his leadership a concern that today does a manufacturing business second in volume only to United States Steel.

Truly it may be said, and with little room for dispute, that his sharp eye for the pennies and nickels and dimes founded a compact, economically efficient industry to supplant a scattered assortment of inefficient, uneconomic small units. The proof of the economic service he performed is in the large financial success, on the narrowest of profit margins, of the business unit he built.

Through his years of working with live stock and meat products and packing he had accumulated a fund of experience—sometimes it seemed to a harassed department head that father's experience must be principally a knowledge of where to look for leaks of money or material. His watchfulness—of which his frequent visits to Bubbly Creek were typical—taught every good man in the organization the need for not wasting a penny. Few pennies, consequently, were wasted.

First thing every morning at the office would come the question, "Any hogs die during the night?" If any had died, there was trouble—enough trouble so that the loss did not occur again soon. He knew that hogs, if they have plenty of room, do not smother. Eventually everyone who had anything to do with the company's hogs knew the same thing. So the hogs were kept in roomy, uncrowded pens—and few were lost from this source.

It was the eye for waste which brought Gustavus Swift from the East to Chicago in 1875. Glamour enveloped the cattle business of fifty and sixty years ago. These were the picturesque days of longhorn herds plodding in fogs of dust across the Great Plains.

Wide-hatted cowmen flanked the herds, yipping and swinging their ropes to drive the strays back into line.

Hundreds of miles the steers were herded, to the end of steel where venturesome railroads pushed their pioneering lines into the West. At the railroad the cattle were driven aboard slatted cars and hauled to the East of concentrated populations which demanded beef above the local ability to supply.

The animals were shipped to central live-stock markets. One of these was at Brighton, just outside Boston; another at Albany; another at Buffalo. At these stockyards the animals were sold and shipped to the slaughterers.

An amount of the glamour of the cattle ranges surrounded even the stockyards—diluted glamour, but glamour nevertheless. For here cattlemen rode from pen to pen, bartered on horseback, and in tall cowhide boots swaggered the streets of the cities.

But beyond the stockyards was little of the glamourous. Unsanitary conditions, thriftless practices, unsound customs prevailed on every hand.

Each community had its little slaughterhouse. Animals beyond the local supply were shipped from the nearest stockyards. They were slaughtered by the local butchers, who sold the meat before it had time to spoil. Refrigerators for keeping meat were almost unknown.

The abattoir was literally a shambles. Meat and hides were the products. Livers, hearts, tongues all went unweighed to the meat market man who bought a whole carcass of beef. Everything else was waste, or at best was used as an unwholesome ration for a sty of "slaughterhouse hogs."[1]

Into this hodge-podge of small, dirty, wasteful local businesses came the Cape Cod Yankee who was to upset practically every idea which had been accepted in the trade since its inception. His acquaintance with meats and live stock had begun in 1855, at the age of fourteen, when he went to work for his brother, a local butcher. It had continued, and grown, through the different phases of slaughterer, local dealer, export cattle shipper, and wholesale meat dealer until at thirty-five he was partner in two large, well-established firms and sole owner of a third,

---

[1] The improvements in sanitation and the development of inspection methods constituted one of G. F. Swift's notable contributions to the preparation of meats for human consumption. His methods, scientifically worked out in the light of scientific discoveries, formed a basis for the inspection and control exercised by the Bureau of Animal Industry of the United States Government. This supervision is extended to over nine hundred packers today, principally those engaged in interstate commerce.

local and smaller enterprise. His interests had spread from Cape Cod to Albany and Buffalo. His firms did business in eastern Massachusetts as well as abroad. He was, as they say down Cape Cod way, getting on in the world.

But Gustavus Franklin Swift was never content simply to get on. Always he saw opportunities ahead for eliminating waste, thereby getting more business and making more money for himself.

At first he saw the waste of buying cattle which had passed through the hands of too many middle-men and against which too many charges had accumulated. He went west to buy the cattle nearer their source, to eliminate these extra charges.

Then he began to think about the waste of shipping the whole animal east instead of shipping only the parts which were needed there. It was not alone the freight on the sixty per cent inedible portion—though that was a tempting saving if it could be attained. But also in shipping the cattle east they were bruised too much. They shrank in weight too much. The expense of feeding in transit was too much. It was all waste—and to my father any waste was too much!

Father was the man who began to slaughter cattle at Chicago, and to ship the beef east. At first this was confined to the winter months. Then, through the refrigerator car's development, it became an all-year business. And thereby the greatest saving possible in producing meat from animals had become

a reality. This saving from that time on meant cheap-
er meat for the consumer, higher prices for the cat-
tleman—and the birth of a great industry.

It was not, of course, as simple as all that. There
were years of venturing, years of back-breaking,
heart-breaking, spirit-breaking work. There were
in those early years times when if G. F. Swift's debts
had been measured against his assets he would have
been unquestionably insolvent.

But his frugality in the management of his business
overcame these handicaps—and left him eventually
in command of one of the greatest businesses of the
world.

How the refrigerator car and the beef cooler were
perfected is a story in itself. Through many a summer's night at his plant he alternately eyed the thermometer in his single beef cooler and ordered his
men to shovel more salt and ice, faster.

Through many years, before the Interstate Commerce Act was passed, he fought single-handed a railroad association which would not haul his dressed
beef at a rate he could pay.

How he wore down the eastern public's prejudice
against western dressed beef is of itself an epic of
selling.

With all of these major problems to handle, however, he never overlooked the economies of operation and the need to develop every possible revenue
from the materials passing through his hands. If
he had lost sight of this, then Swift & Company could

hardly have survived the early years to remain in business successfully today.

In the free-and-easy days of slaughtering in New England, for example, the slaughterer saved, besides the meat and the hide, only the head, feet, tripe, heart, liver, and tongue. The head, feet, and tripe constituted a "set," and a set was sold separately. If the customer bought a whole carcass, he received free a heart, tongue, and liver.

On the outskirts of the larger slaughterhouses, such as that of Anthony, Swift & Company at Fall River, there grew up the establishments of people, who, while the slaughterers blindly followed the age-old customs, made money out of what the meat men threw away. The butchers were glad to have this "rubbish" carted off, for disposing of it was difficult.

The by-products people made a good thing of it. The big firm in the trade which included such products as neat's foot oil, tripe, and so on was also operating extensively in some of the materials which it did not have to pay for because they were not included in the sets which had a market value.

Shortly after my father came to Chicago and began operating on the larger scale which characterized most of the Chicago dressed-meat establishments, he was instrumental in developing paying outlets for other by-products. By-products revenue is what developed his business.

A man was brought on from Fall River who contracted for sausage casings at a stipulated figure per

UNION STOCKYARDS OF CHICAGO IN 1865.

carcass. Blood and tankage became a source of fertilizer. We made a hobby, almost, of fertilizer and a few years later of oleomargarine. In our early days at Chicago, by-products people bought the sets, the blood and tankage, and the shin-bones for knife handles. Peddlers were encouraged who came to buy livers and sell them from their wagons in the poorer parts of town. What livers could not be disposed of in more profitable ways were tanked. Nothing was given away—this would have been waste.

G. F. Swift knew, by Cape Cod instinct, that no enterprise can grow soundly and survive the lean days which always come, unless it blocks off every possible source of waste. Even though a customer might be induced to buy a whole carcass instead of only three quarters, by "throwing in" heart, liver, and tongue, it would not increase that customer's sale of meat. His retail customers could be counted on to eat just the same amount of meat; and if he bought the smaller quantity he would simply have to come back that much sooner to replenish his stock. Hence, if the heart, liver, and tongue could be sold separately, and made to yield some of the money the new packer needed so urgently, then certainly they must yield it.

Before he had finished with the process, he was using everything from the animal to produce a profit. In fact, the hackneyed remark that Chicago packers use every part of the hog but the squeal probably had its inception in a remark my father once made, when the by-products utilization was complete, that "Now we use all of the hog except his grunt."

Not that Swift & Company was the only one to do anything along the lines of by-products. All of the sizable packers were at work on the problem. The keen competition among them all, and especially among the larger concerns, forced down prices and forced down margins. Unless one kept abreast of the others in by-products utilization, then that laggard inevitably went under.

G. F. Swift was without question the aggressor in this war for extra sources of revenue. He was never satisfied with his business. He knew he could get more if he could crowd his prices below the rest of the field without sacrificing his profit. Out of this continual pushing for sales by cutting his costs, he built his own business to a place of preeminence.

After the stage of selling raw materials to others to make products from, came the stage where our own people did the jobs themselves and thus crowded costs down a little more.

New lines were entered; by-products were split into further by-products; and out of it all, the public benefited as well as we did.

Along with the development of by-products revenue—ahead of it, in fact, for it required no development of processes—he practiced this creed of keeping every expense at rock-bottom. Swift & Company had a reputation wherever it was known, as a thrifty, compact, well-managed business. There were no little cracks in the walls which permitted anything to get away undetected.

One of father's especial ways to hold down expense was to avoid alterations which, while desirable, were not necessary. He hated to see mechanics at work around any of his properties. The sight of a man with a hammer or a saw or a trowel was a red flag to him.

"Whenever you see a lot of mechanics at work anywhere you are in charge, fire 'em," were the instructions he once gave a man whom he had placed over a considerable section of the company's properties.

"But sometimes they are needed, Mr. Swift," protested the department head.

"They'll find their way back, then," he disposed of this argument. "They're a luxury. We can't afford luxuries. It isn't only the high wages you pay 'em—it's the lumber and nails and brick and hardware they use, too. No, sir, when you see a gang of 'em around and you don't know that you have to have 'em, be on the safe side and fire 'em. That's the way I always work it."

After all, there is little question that his ideas were fundamentally right in regard to holding down expenses. Given an enterprise which has an economic reason for its existence, then if you stop every leak, that enterprise is bound to be in good shape. It is the leaks which ruin more basically sound businesses than any other cause. For one business man who watches expenses carefully, there are five who are careless. And of fifty who are careful, not more than one really keeps his organization keyed up to the importance of waste as did G. F. Swift.

He was visiting the St. Joseph plant back in the '90s, shortly after it had been built. As he was going over the plant with the manager, he noticed a place where car loaders had spiked a loading runway to the dock. When the runway had been removed, the nails had been left sticking up from the planking.

"Nice dock you have there," he observed casually.

"Yes, fine, isn't it?" agreed the manager.

"But look at those nails"—pointing to them. "You won't have a dock if you let 'em do that."

They walked along and father began looking at some other parts of the plant with the superintendent, who had been a few feet behind all the while. The manager meanwhile encountered one of the office boys in the yard and sent word by him to the loading foreman that those nails must be removed within five minutes.

On the way back, the chief led the party quite casually along the loading dock. This time he was with the superintendent. And while he appeared to be unaware, the manager saw him looking for the nails and scraping about a bit with his foot in the vain effort to find them. Finally the rest of the party was allowed to go on its way, while the manager was taken to the cooler to look at the beef.

Together they looked over the carcasses for

perhaps ten minutes without a word. Then: "Did you have those nails pulled out?"

"Yes, Mr. Swift."

"Well," plaintively, "I wish you wouldn't have things fixed up until after I'm off the plant. How do you think I'm going to make everybody look alive about these things if you get 'em fixed up before I have a chance to tell the other men about them?"

When the St. Joseph plant was being built, he would go there about once a month. Ostensibly his visits were to check up on the general progress of construction. There was a vigorous idea among some of the men in charge of construction, however, that he came out quite as much to see that everyone was working as hard as he should.

He appeared one mid-morning at construction headquarters. No one had known that he was in St. Joseph. But from his comments it was apparent that he had arrived early and had been on a self-conducted tour of the plant.

"There's a gang of carpenters over on the hog-house," was his opening shot. "Of about twenty men, not more than half a dozen are really working. I think you need a new foreman for them, to get the work out of 'em. And something is the matter with the bricklaying gang; they haven't got enough hodcarriers to keep the masons busy. Somebody better take care of that in a hurry. If more of the bosses were out on the job instead of in the office, this plant would go up for a whole lot less money."

After that, there was less chair warming!

Whenever he visited a branch house or plant, he went without warning. Generally he came in the back way and got his eyes full of what was going on, before ever he looked up the men in charge.

Watchmen were almost a hobby with him. He wanted them alert, on the job, and not to be talked out of doing their duty. One story which has almost become a classic among the men who knew him has to do with a visit he made to the East St. Louis plant.

He appeared at the back gate one morning and tried to walk past. "Here," challenged the watchman, "where are you going?"

"Isn't this Swift & Company's plant?" he inquired.

"Yes, but you can't come in this way. Have to go around the front," directed the watchman.

"I'm going in this way," he declared, to see what the watchman would do.

"No, you're not," the man contradicted him.

"I certainly am. It's shorter to go through than to go around."

"You won't go through this gate," the watchman announced flatly. "Now, get along out of here."

"Say, do you know who I am? I'm G. F. Swift."

"I don't care who you are. My orders are that nobody comes through here unless it's part of his job. You can't go through here, even if you are Mr. Swift—and I don't think you are."

"What's your name?"

"Bateman."

"All right, Bateman, you'll hear more of this."
And he started for the front gate.

A few minutes later he appeared at the manager's
desk. He apparently had something on his mind,
and he was not long getting it off. "You've got a
watchman named Bateman on the back gate?"

"Yes, sir."

"Mighty good man. He wouldn't let me in. Better raise his wages. A man like that will save us a
whole lot more than he costs."

There was another time when, in the sweet pickle
cellar at Chicago, a new watchman found him poking
into the barrels and examining the meats. The watchman ordered him out.

"All right," said the chief, without identifying
himself. But as soon as the watchman's back was
turned he resumed his looking.

In a minute the watchman returned. "Here, I
told you you can't do that. You'll have to go out,
right away." So, with all apparent grace, the founder of the business started out.

But on the way he saw something else which attracted his attention. It was not thirty seconds before
the employee had him by the arm—a valiant thing
to do, since father towered well above six feet while
the watchman was a scant five feet six. "Look here,"
was the man's ultimatum. "I've told you to get out
of here, twice. And you're still hanging around.
Now get out before I put you out."

Again the boss did as he was told—but this time

he went all the way. Within the week that employee was getting two dollars more in every pay envelope. And father never tired of telling the story. To his mind, it illustrated the very qualities of carefulness and persistence which he most desired in his men.

One characteristic which seemed almost a peculiarity, though actually it was a necessity in conserving his attention for the jobs that needed him most, was his disinclination to talk about departments which were making a profit. "I have no time to talk about that," he would point out to anyone who might undertake it. "I want to talk about the ones that are losing. I have no time for the others."

No detail was too small to be worth watching, if it bore on the subject of waste. He used to keep an eye out for Swift wagons on the streets and when he saw a meat wagon, one quick glance told him whether the meat was properly covered.

If it was not, he was out in the street in a jump. The driver was called down off his seat, then and there to be shown exactly how meat should be covered. It is said that he never had to stop the same man twice—and in later years he rarely had to stop any wagons. Swift meat went out completely covered by the tarpaulin. Everyone who had anything to do with the teaming had heard it too often to forget it.

When the business was getting started, he used to check over every detail himself. One plant man tells of being called up to the chief's desk about the amount of beef which had been put into a car. "See here," he was taken to task, "your sheets show so much beef put into car number thus-and-so for this branch house. The branch house sales sheets show three hundred and fifty pounds more beef sold out of that car than you say you put in it. That means one beef went in without being tallied. We can't have that sort of thing happening. It might not have been shipped to one of our own branches." He watched everything as closely as that.

A good many years later, when he could no longer check all things himself, he still insisted on seeing the facts of every claim. Always he had on his desk several claim sheets with the name in each instance of the employee who had made the error. And until the business had grown far beyond the point where anyone else might have relinquished this, he used to talk personally with every man who made one of these errors. The interviews were usually none too pleasant—yet they were talks where the man was taught rather than threatened. And anyone who was called in because he made a claim error took away from G. F. Swift's desk a comprehension of why errors and wastes cannot be allowed, if a business is to go ahead to success and profit.

Once, on a visit to a western plant, he headed straight for the oil house when the superintendent started out with him to go over the place. As soon as he was in the oil house, he asked that the sewer board be taken up. And the sewer, sure enough, revealed a loss of oil stock. He followed up the line until he came to the cooler from which this sewer drained. His inspection showed the tierces were leaky.

The foreman was sent for. But he was not given simply a general reprimand on the subject of waste. He was told, besides the fact that the oil was worth money, that a shipment from this plant to Rotterdam had arrived with many of the tierces empty. He heard about the freight, both rail and ocean. He heard about the effect which a shipment of this sort has on a customer who is expecting the shipment for immediate use. Altogether it was a lesson in business which any foreman might be glad of the opportunity to receive.

An amusing sequel was that several months afterwards on father's next visit to this plant word got ahead of him to the foreman. So the foreman shut off the sewer, had it cleaned out and then forgot to open it again.

Once more the visitor came in and had the floor board lifted. And to his astonishment he found the sewer not only free from oil, but also free from the water it should have been carrying. This time the lecture was not so restrained in tone.

In his zeal for eliminating the needless expenses, he would spare himself no more than anyone else. In going through a hog killing department one day, he had to climb up a dirty ladder. He soiled his hands, and an overzealous boy who accompanied the party to carry the frocks handed the chief a piece of cheesecloth to wipe his hands.

The boss examined the cloth with interest. "What did it cost? How much is in it?" he demanded.

"A cent and three-quarters a yard," the superintendent told him. "There are about four yards of it in that piece."

"Thank you, I will use my own handkerchief," was the instant decision. "I think you should see that the company's supplies are not wasted."

He was always teaching. His aim was not to make a man feel bad for something which had gone to waste, but rather to avoid the possibility of repeating any similar loss. Whether it was a lump of coal which he saw projecting from the cinders in the yard, or whether it was seven cents worth of cheesecloth, he always commented because he wanted his men to realize the importance of the trifles.

One result was expressed in his own words, "I don't have to go out and hire very many managers. I can raise better than I can hire." It is noteworthy that today, twenty-odd years after his death, most of the men in positions of high responsibility are men who were trained directly under the founder of the business.

His plan assured him soundly trained managers. Another important result, from his point of view, was that it avoided the tendency to five-figured salaries, which his business could not afford in the early days.

A man who has been brought up from the ranks through all of the different stages in one company is almost certain to be a better man for that company than a man who is hired from the outside. Moreover, such a man realizes that he has invested a great deal of his time in the employing company, just as it has in him. He recognizes that loyalty is mutual and that there is on him an obligation to the company just as the company has an obligation to him.

Such a man is a living refutation of the theory that the only currency which can enter into the employee-employer relation is that of cash down at the moment. He recognizes that the man who has come up through the ranks has a greater opportunity to be worth a big salary and a big responsibility in future than has the outsider. And in the long run, he is right.

My father inspired this loyalty in his men. They knew him as the man who had taught them what they knew about the business, the man who had built the business and had given them correspondingly more opportunity for advancement than if the company had gone ahead with less phenomenal strides.

They had seen him recognize, in a material way, the employer's obligation to his men. They acknowledged their obligation to him, as well as their personal loyalty to him as a man.

It was well for him and for the business that they did. For despite the years of unparalleled prosperity which had come to the company after it had gained a bit of headway, there was coming a lean time. The business had grown fast. If it had failed to come through the times of trouble, the verdict must be that it had grown too fast. As it is, one must say that it had grown to the absolute limit of safety.

CHAPTER II

"WE CANNOT FAIL!"

FROM his first transaction as a boy until some time after the wearing days of 1893, my father never had enough cash to handle his volume of business comfortably.

It was not that he did not have during most of this time a good deal of capital to work with. Rather, his vision of the opportunities in his business ran far ahead of the money which the business earned him. And his daring led him to expand abreast of his vision rather than abreast of his cash.

He was a born expansionist. But if he had lacked this tendency, his first few years of shipping beef east in refrigerator cars would have implanted it in him. For, just as soon as he had succeeded in delivering his Chicago-dressed beef all sweet and edible in the hungry centers of the East, he was able to undersell everyone else.

No one could haul live cattle east, slaughter them there, and sell the meat for anything like what it was costing us to lay down Chicago beef at the same point. We were not paying freight on the inedible portions of the animals, nor feeding them for another thousand miles of railroad journey and standing a heavy shrinkage in shipment to boot.

24

The first working capital which G. F. Swift had was the twenty-five dollars his father gave him when he was sixteen to serve the double purpose of keeping him from going to Boston for a job and of setting him up in the meat business. He got this twenty-five dollars in 1855. He expanded it to a good deal more by shrewd trading and hard work.

In 1873 he was "well fixed," as the New England idiom has it. And despite that panic year's losses to the three firms in which he had interests, he was getting on in the world.

Yet within three years, so thoroughly was he convinced of the opportunities ahead, he shifted his scene of operations to Chicago from eastern Massachusetts. Shifted his ideas from eastern slaughtering to Chicago-dressed beef. And held so firmly to these ideas that his Boston partner, James A. Hathaway, forced a dissolution of their partnership.

Hathaway was the financial man, Gustavus Swift the live-stock man, of the firm of Hathaway & Swift. Its operations had been financially comfortable because Hathaway had both money and belief in his younger partner's ability.

But when it came to so radical a change as my father proposed, the older man would have none of it. Partnership dissolved, my father received his share shortly after he came to Chicago.

The proceeds to him were a little more than thirty thousand dollars. It was all the money he had, and it did not look to him to be very much. He had been operating three sizable businesses—and even in those days live cattle cost about one thousand dollars a car.

He had no illusions that he could work comfortably on this amount of money. But he did not let this fact deter him.

No one saw fit to give him much competition in the early days at Chicago. The general attitude around the Yards was that if the Yankee newcomer was allowed enough rope he would hang himself. His logical competitors, the big Chicago concerns engaged in pork packing and in the local fresh meat business—the concerns which were his real competitors when their owners finally saw how wholly right were his ideas—let him have so much rope that instead of hanging himself he obtained a substantial lead.

The savings through dressing beef in Chicago instead of shipping live cattle east constituted so large a sum per head that Swift beef, which was better than locally slaughtered beef, could be sold below the market and still leave a handsome margin. Once the plan was working, we made money at a great rate.

Obviously he could not count on the rest of the world to leave him this rich field. Some day the other members of the industry would realize what was going on. And forthwith they would enter into competition to obtain a share of the eastern business.

Under these circumstances my father did the only

thing thinkable. He went to any length to expand his business while he had the field to himself.

He borrowed every cent he could to build more refrigerator cars, to extend his plant, to establish his distributing machinery in the East. Every cent his business yielded went back into it again.

Friends in the East, former associates and competitors, were induced to buy shares in his enterprise. And so it was that by the time the big Chicago pork packers awakened to the profit for them in fresh beef he was intrenched as firmly as they. Financially, that is. In the beef business he had a head start which was never to be lost.

But his head start was stalwartly contested. The other concerns, once they entered the race, worked for business. There was plenty to be had—what the local slaughterers of the East had had but could no longer hold against the economically invulnerable competition from Chicago.

Our problem was finding the money to build the equipment necessary for getting the business which was to be had. Obviously, if we were first on the ground in a given territory we should always be the big factor there while the other concerns would be merely our competitors. And father was a great one for being the big factor in anything he touched.

On April 1, 1885, Swift & Company was incorporated for $300,000. On December 1, 1886, the capital stock was increased to $3,000,000—the inventory showed that the plant was worth it. December

1, 1891, saw an increase to $5,000,000. Shortly after-
wards still more stock was sold, for a total capitalization of $7,500,000.

The first issue of stock had gone pretty much to
eastern friends and associates—wholesale meat dealers, retail butchers, and live-stock shippers for export.
After a short while, Swift shares were universally
recognized as desirable securities. They were always
sold directly by the company to investors, merely by
announcing the new issue and giving "rights" to the
shareholders of record. Every share of stock ever
sold by the company has been sold for its par value.

When the panic of 1893 swept down upon the man
in charge of the business, as it swept down upon all
the commerce of the nation, he was not ready for it.
He was at the height of his last big period of expanding the business. Swift plants were springing up
along the Missouri River—for if it was good to dress
beef at Chicago and save hauling live cattle a thousand miles, was it not better to dress it at Kansas City
and save fifteen hundred? The new plants increased
the earnings, but also they increased the capital
requirements. Hence when the panic came, money
was tight with us.

My father had always regarded his credit, and
rightly so, as unquestionably his greatest asset. When
a loan came due, he always had the money on the
spot—and he usually asked for a renewal immediately after he had paid.

His credit was wonderfully good. No wonder.

In the first place he had been building, from his earliest days, this unbroken record of prompt payment. Then there was his history of commercial success. And not least of all was his personality.

Anyone meeting Gustavus F. Swift was at once impressed with the fundamental honesty of him. It was in his face, in his manner, in his whole personality. One knew, instinctively, that here was a man to be trusted to any extreme. And besides his whole air of honesty, there was no question that he was substantial. Physically, he was over six feet and weighed about a hundred and ninety. There was no suggestion of fatness about him; he was bone and muscle. His whole appearance was enough to lend money on!

When he first came to the Chicago Yards, the East was his source of all funds. Chiefly they were derived from cattle and meat sources, from men who knew him in the stockyards and meat centers of New England. And through these people he was able to get substantial lines of credit from eastern banks, both through personal calls and by correspondence. Swift paper was, in 1893, scattered throughout the East; almost every bank in New England and New York State had some.

The large banks, too, in Chicago and other centers had Swift notes in more substantial amounts. Yet even at this time he felt himself held back by the lack of money. He *was* so held back; his vision raced ahead so fast that the money could not keep pace. His maxim was to borrow all the money anyone would lend him. He never turned down the offer of a loan. The business was growing too fast for that.

The business was, it may parenthetically be admitted, growing at a rate faster than was altogether conservative. As I have said, he was a natural-born expansionist. And for years all of his training had been for more expansion, and then still more beyond that.

We went into the panic, in May of 1893, owing about $10,000,000 to the banks—a tidy sum in those days. Forthwith the banks evinced the greatest desire to collect their loans and not to renew them.

Here was the test of G. F. Swift's policy. Could he pay off these loans, accumulate enough new borrowed money in hard times to carry on his business, and emerge unscathed? Or would he find himself in financial difficulties which must result in money loss, perhaps even in loss of the management of the business? These questions were very real—for in 1893 ten million dollars was not a sum to be bandied lightly about, nor for that matter is it today.

Those who knew my father best say that in his life were dozens of occasions when almost anyone else in the world would have quit, but when he fought his way through the difficulties by sheer grit. Of all of these occasions, 1893 takes first place.

For several months then, he literally did not know two days in advance just where he was going to get the money with which to meet his obligations. Times were hard, hard as ever they had been in the memory of man. Collections came only through everlasting persistence and even then they could not be relied on. Several times the day was saved by expedients which could have been devised by no one less determined than was Gustavus F. Swift that his business would not fail to meet its obligations, and promptly.

Off and on, rumors became current that Swift and Company had failed or was about to fail. Always this was the signal for another lot of creditors to descend for assurances. And always they received the assurances that all was well, just as they always received their money on the dot.

The president of one Chicago bank heard these rumors and became badly worried. So he called at the office, bearing a statement showing all of Swift & Company's notes in his bank with amounts and due dates. The head of the business looked over the list. Then he said:

"I am sorry, sir, that you put your bookkeeper to the trouble of making out this long statement. Are any of these notes due?"

"No, Mr. Swift. But I am worried about the rumors I have heard about Swift & Company's financial condition."

"I have always thought it was a pretty good man who could pay his debts when they came due," declared my father. "And I have a record of always having paid every debt when it came due. These notes will all be paid when they come due, but I can't pay you before then. You will get your money on time." And he did.

Gustavus Franklin Swift believed in the destiny of his business. He sincerely believed that it could not fail, for he would not let it. A dozen or more times that summer the company could not have met its obligations except for the superhuman efforts of its founder.

Practically every department head of the company had lent the company his lifetime savings on a note endorsed by G. F. Swift. Many of the subordinate employees had lent their money, too. Some of these loans were well up into five figures; others were of only a few hundreds of dollars. But every one of them was made voluntarily. The men knew their chief needed cash, so they brought him what they could.

The aggregate of these loans by employees was large. The margin of safety by which the company escaped disaster was, several times, extremely narrow—much narrower than the margin given by the loans of employees. If Swift people had not lent their own money, the business might not have come through.

Small loans were made not only by employees but also by outside friends and associates. Many a live-stock commission man in the yards had lent ten thousand or even twenty-five thousand dollars on an endorsed note. Every cent of the family's was in the business then.

But my father gathered in money not only from these logical sources; he also brought in some goodly sums from places of which no one else might have thought. One morning, bright and early, he sent for the department head in charge of ice houses and icing stations. "Do you know A. S. Piper?" he demanded.

"Yes, I know him rather well."

"I see by the paper that he had a big fire in one of his ice houses. The paper says it was fully insured, and that it was worth a hundred thousand dollars."

"Yes, I think the ice house was worth fully one hundred thousand dollars, Mr. Swift And Mr. Piper would not slip up on a question like insurance."

"Hm-m," his boss concluded. "That hundred thousand is too much money for him to have."

"He can handle one hundred thousand dollars very intelligently, Mr. Swift."

"He can't handle it as well as I can," was the retort. "Can you get him to come to my office?"

Within an hour or two the department head had Mr. Piper in the big front office. And then, as the eyewitness has since recounted the story, was displayed an urbane, an almost ingratiating manner which seldom came to the surface.

"I have heard a great deal about you, Mr. Piper," he told his visitor. "Lots of people will no doubt come to you about this hundred thousand dollars which the fire insurance companies will pay you.

The place for it is with Swift & Company, at six per cent interest. I will give you a demand note, and will endorse it personally. Then you can get your money when you want it."

He got the money! The department head ushered Mr. Piper to his carriage, and returned to his own desk. An hour or two later his chief sent for him. "I suppose you thought I wouldn't get that money," he chuckled.

"Yes, sir, that's exactly what I thought."

"Well, I had to have it. I suppose that if you needed that hundred thousand, you'd just sit around and say you couldn't get it."

"I don't know, Mr. Swift. I probably would have tried."

"I'll tell you, young man, you've never needed money the way I needed that money. If you had, you'd know just how I felt about it. You'd have got it too."

Every morning during these times of stress there was laid on his desk a sheet showing estimated money requirements and estimated receipts. Those documents were the storm center of the business.

The estimated requirements were inelastic. If a note came due, it came due and that was all there was to it. Live stock had to be purchased, for customers must be supplied with fresh meat.

Estimated receipts were, however, highly elastic. Their natural elasticity consisted principally of their tendency to shrink. Customers were not paying their bills as promptly as in other times; many of them were in straits which resulted in their eventual failure.

To offset this natural shortage was my father's big task. For only too often the estimated receipts fell perilously short of the requirements, and the actual receipts fell short of the estimates. Then it was that he accomplished strokes such as the hundred-thousand-dollar loan from A. S. Piper.

His task was complicated by the thick-flying rumors of bankruptcy. One prominent company in the industry had failed. Bankers sat on the edges of their chairs, awaiting the next failure.

And because Swift & Company had expanded so fast and was spread out so thin, it seemed the logical candidate.

G. F. Swift's handling of the whole situation revealed to the pessimistic bankers a consummate financial skill of which they had never suspected him. For the whole summer, while the panic raged, he drove coolly along the edge of a cliff above it. Sometimes he had one wheel part-way over. If ever he had lost his head, if ever he had become careless, he must have crashed squarely into it. How he ran along tranquilly, getting the money somehow on the day he had to have it and meeting every obligation on the dot, is one of the wonder points in business history. Certainly it was the height of his accomplishment.

Tranquilly? Almost always. But there were one

or two occasions when even his outward tranquility was disturbed.

One of these was at the time when the ticker tape from the Chicago Board of Trade carried the message that Swift & Company had failed. Inside half an hour he was on the floor of the board, a place he had probably not been half a dozen times in his life. He strode in the door, walked to a table and rapped on it with that hard, heavy fist of his. Everyone looked up except a few traders off in a far corner, so he called, "Attention! Attention!"

By this time he had the floor. He raised his voice so that everyone could hear clearly what he had to say: "It is reported that Swift & Company has failed. Swift & Company has not failed. Swift & Company cannot fail!" He walked out in a dead silence which held for thirty seconds after he was gone.

Another time he got word that a meeting of bankers had been called to consider just what steps should be taken to put an end to all this uncertainty and to plan concerted demands at once so heavy he could not possibly meet them.

Twenty minutes later any passer-by on Michigan Avenue might have seen him whipping his carriage horse through the crowded traffic as though he had the street to himself. The least surprised man present, he walked into the midst of the bankers' meeting which had gathered to bury the business.

He opened up without wasting any time: "You gentlemen think you might be better off by bringing financial pressure to bear on us. I'm sorry, gentlemen, but we have to have more money, not less. It is up to you to lend it to us. If we don't get it, we go down—and a good many of you go down with us."

Before he left the meeting, he had increased his line of credit—and on terms which permitted of no future harassment. The bankers who had met to call his loans increased them!

Yet nothing can make me believe that if he had failed with these men, my father would not have succeeded in raising enough money somewhere or other to meet any demands which could be made on him. When he told the Board of Trade, "Swift & Company cannot fail," he was telling what he felt to be the truth. When he told the bankers, "If we don't get more money, we go down," he was telling what he knew they believed and what would therefore give him the greatest leverage on them for increased loans.

Periodically, even today, one hears or reads how this or that packer poured millions of dollars into Swift & Company in 1893 in order to save a gigantic failure. To the man who does not know the competitive situation which existed at that time, this may sound reasonable. To anyone who was in the heart of the industry at that time it is ridiculous. If we had gone out of existence, or had even suspended operations, it would have meant millions of dollars in increased annual sales to each of the large packers. That statement should make the situation clear.

Actually, during the whole period, Swift & Company had exactly one bit of assistance from another packer. When he saw ahead a shortage of money rather more stringent than even the regular daily crisis, father arranged that Morris & Company should pay for Swift & Company's purchases of live stock in the Chicago stockyards for a period of not exceeding one week.

As it worked out, Morris & Company paid for two days' purchases by Swift & Company on the Chicago market—a sum not over one hundred thousand dollars at the most. On the third day the "estimated receipts" were bettered by the actual receipts, and Morris & Company was repaid in full on that day.

This was not a situation where Swift & Company would have fallen by the wayside if the hundred thousand dollars had not been forthcoming. A simple way, but less desirable, would have been to suspend purchasing live stock for a day or two and shut down the packing house.

Not only did we weather the storm, but also we operated continuously throughout—though at a reduced rate of production because of the need for liquidating inventories. My father insisted that he had to keep the packing houses open, even though money was so hard to get. He declared he would not willingly be caught short of product—and he wasn't.

But there was a time in '93 when the shelves were almost bare of all stock—by-products, glue, hides, wool, pickled and smoked meats—everything that could be sold for cash. The head of the business kept firmly to the idea that if you needed money, there was no point in holding goods in an effort to avoid a loss. He needed money right then more than he needed anything else; he sold off everything which would yield money. This is how he provided the funds to pay off those banks which were clamoring for cash.

At the beginning of the panic, in May, we owed about ten million dollars to banks. By September, when the worst of the storm was past, the bank loans had been reduced to one million—and this was in the banks which had proved themselves ready and willing to believe in G. F. Swift. Given another month of the panic, he unquestionably could have liquidated every cent of bank indebtedness. As it was, the actual accomplishment was a feat little short of unbelievable.

Yet, except for the one or two occasions when anyone would have lapsed from tranquility, he handled the whole job quietly, comfortably, and efficiently. It was World's Fair year and the house was full of visitors all summer. On a Saturday morning in June he called in his chief clerk in charge of banking matters and announced, "I am going away. I don't want to see you again until Monday." And he went out to his buggy.

Within half an hour the head of one of the large downtown banks telephoned. He wanted to talk with the chief; but after failing to get him, or one of several other people, he talked with the financial clerk. "There is a rumor downtown that Swift & Company has failed and I must get hold of Mr. Swift very quickly," he told the employee. "Even if he is away, you find him and get this word to him."

The clerk had a feeling that his boss was at the World's Fair. So he set out for the Midway, and walked around looking for the familiar tall figure. Finally, at about 1:30, he found him.

His boss listened to his excited story. Then he smiled. "I said I didn't want to see you until Monday. I meant it. The bank is closed, isn't it, until Monday? All right, we'll answer them on Monday." With no more ado he continued on his way.

For while he was tremendously concerned about his firm's credit, he would never allow anyone else's excitement to stampede him. He personally instructed the handful of employees in the banking department that the duty of the department and of everyone in it was to keep the company's credit good. He kept his finger on all of it.

Long after he was running a large and widely ramified business, after he had relinquished to subordinates duties which are supremely important, he still held to the details of the credit structure. He signed all notes, warehouse receipts, and other documents of like nature. He was able to present a full statement of the company's financial condition from the records which he maintained.

One evening early in the panic year the president

of a large bank wrote asking for a statement of his assets and liabilities—something which was a good deal less freely given out by all concerns then than now. The request arrived by messenger after office hours.

Next morning he appeared at the bank with a statement made out in his own writing. The statement showed that while the firm owed a large sum, it was a long way from insolvency. He went over the statement with the bank president and left it with him.

Then he went to another bank and to another, until he had been to all five of the banks where he had considerable amounts borrowed. To each bank president, after the first, he said just about this: "You did not ask for this, but another bank did. I gave it a statement and I want to deal fairly. I have brought you one also. I hope it will be satisfactory."

He afterwards explained to someone who questioned the wisdom of this move: "There's no use in trying to deal with a banker and not letting him know how you stand. If I had not always worked that way, I would not have received as good support as I did receive from the banks during the panic. And if I had not submitted that statement when the first bank asked for it, there probably would have been a good deal harder situation a little later on than actually ever developed."

Years before, when he was doing much of his own cattle-buying, the market broke in the East—this was in the very early days when he was still shipping cattle, before he was slaughtering in Chicago. He saw an opportunity, with the consequent cheap prices in the Chicago Yards, to get hold of a great many cattle and start them rolling eastward while everyone else at Chicago was holding off in trepidation. That would mean a nice profit the next week, when the cattle could be sold in a strong eastern market.

So he bought and bought and bought some more. His weight tickets, which are a form of document constituting a sight draft payable at the buyer's bank, came rolling into the National Livestock Bank in great quantities.

Levi B. Doud was president of the bank. When the flood of tickets reached a disturbing height, he sent a boy out to bring in G. F. Swift. But that gentleman did not come to the bank. Instead, he kept right on buying cattle. A second boy failed to bring him in and a third. So Doud got on his horse and hunted up the recalcitrant customer. He found him on horseback, at the cattle pens.

"You're buying a lot of cattle, Mr. Swift," was his greeting.

"I know it," agreed my father. "Weigh 'em," he said to a live-stock commission man he was with, to indicate that he was buying this lot too.

"To tell you the truth, your tickets have overdrawn your credit. I'm worrying about you, Mr. Swift."

"Glad to hear it," declared his customer heartily. "I was worrying a little myself until now, but there's no use of two of us worrying. I'm not worrying any more. Good-by, Mr. Doud. I've got to go over and look at some cattle." And he rode away.

That was perhaps a method not to be advocated in dealing with bankers generally. But he knew his man. In '93, he was on the ragged edge of his credit with Levi B. Doud almost every day.

A good many times during a few months his weight tickets represented a large share of the money in the National Livestock Bank. He would be far overdrawn at night. But Doud knew him as well as he knew Doud. There was a world of mutual confidence, after all the years of dealing.

So, after 3:00 p.m., when the day's tickets were in, G. F. Swift and his chief clerk would go over to see Doud. The three would sit down and figure out just where they stood. Then, somehow or other, they would devise a way to leave Swift's account in satisfactory shape overnight. Next day, bright and early, part of the morning mail receipts of money would be deposited—and all was well again until three o'clock.

There were key banks of this kind to which he looked for considerable sums and unusual helpfulness. But a large bulk of his financial safety lay in the fact that Swift paper was scattered in small pieces all through the East, which at that time was the only money-lending section of the country. Hardly a bank east of Ohio and north of Virginia which did not have a Swift note or two—whether it was a large bank with five hundred thousand dollars or a small bank with fifteen hundred. But in the widely scattered indebtedness lay an unlikelihood of its all being called at the same time.

The financial and credit-building methods all had to be developed by my father from his own experience and common sense. He had no skilled financial man until L. A. Carton, an established dealer in commercial paper, came in as treasurer along in the latter part of 1893. By that time, G. F. Swift had had about all he wanted of financing for the rest of his life. So he brought in L. A. Carton as a man he could depend on to take over this important job.

L. A. Carton's unusual ability in financing was of very real value from the start. He aided his chief both by taking off his overburdened shoulders the whole responsibility of the corporation's finance and by bringing to this work his specialized financial skill.

There is little question that we had been expanding rather faster than was altogether wise when safety is considered—though this is contrary to the views of Carton that my father's knowledge of every factor in the industry was so great that what to others seemed too fast an expansion really was not. But L. A. Carton, with his skill in corporation finance, saw that thenceforth it might be preferable to go more slowly. He began to exert a conservative influence.

The bigness of his financial operations had come upon father so fast that he hardly realized their magnitude until the panic of 1893 struck. One of the old-timers among the executives often tells how his chief remarked to him, on the first day that the business reached the new high-water mark of one hundred head of cattle, "If I could only kill a hundred cattle a day regularly, that would be about as big a business as I could ask." Yet in less than six months the killing gang was not allowed to start work in the morning unless a hundred cattle were on hand.

To this same man, G. F. Swift remarked when Swift & Company was incorporated for three hundred thousand dollars in 1885, "It seems like an awful lot of money, but we may need it yet." Just twenty months later the capitalization was increased to three millions—because it was needed.

It was the great speed of growth which caught him unawares in 1893. He knew more money was needed for capital. A new issue of stock was offered to the stockholders.

But it did not go. They were already feeling the pinch of the approaching panic. So was begun the long, hard fight which could not really be counted as over until the banks opened their credit resources once more and the new stock issue cleared out in a hurry.

If G. F. Swift had not done everything exactly right, all the way through those stormy months, he must have gone under. But he did everything exactly right. This was a characteristic of his—and a characteristic of the men who made good with him.

CHAPTER III

JUST RIGHT OR ALL WRONG

MANY a man of equal ability has left behind to witness his prowess no such structure as my father left. I have no doubt that many such men have consciously chosen not to. As between a career of undivided attention to business and a life rounded out by a catholicity of interests, they have selected the broader. For them it means greater contentment.

No such choice was thinkable to G. F. Swift. With never a backward look of regret for those pleasures of life which by his choice he perforce left untasted, he unhesitatingly elected to be master of his own business. The cost was more than other men might willingly pay. His whole mind and heart and strength went into building up his packing enterprise. Church and family alone excepted, he had little time or inclination left for outside interests.

Had he been less than unusually able, he could not have succeeded so well in accomplishing his purpose. Yet ability could not by itself have done what he did. His thoroughness was the source of his magic-working dissatisfaction with half measures. Father could not be happy if anything with which he was connected functioned short of one hundred per cent.

Whether it was the way the beef was dressed, or

the salt slush left on icy walks by a careless plant engineer—he would go to the root of the trouble and do his best to correct it for all time to come. On both of these subjects I have heard him deliver repeated lectures to employees. And I cite them not because they were hobbies, but as random selections to typify the range over which his attention wandered.

He was a crank on doing things right, or at least some of his men thought him so. Actually, of course, he had so complete a comprehension of every detail from buying the cattle to running a wholesale market that he saw not only the error but also the ultimate consequence of it.

He recognized that no business can ever attain perfection in all of its operations. But he was determined that his own should come as close to that goal as could any. It is my sincere conviction that he carried his determination over into the realm of accomplishment.

When he found grease in the East St. Louis plant's oil-house sewer, he visualized the irate oleomargarine maker in Rotterdam sputtering guttural expletives because many casks of the shipment he had counted on to keep his plant running had leaked themselves empty in transit. When he observed an Austrian bruise-trimmer doing slovenly work at Kansas City, he appreciated how this must lower the customer's opinion of Swift beef—and to him it made no difference whether that quarter of beef was destined for the epicure of Beacon Hill or the Italian family of South Boston. The inividual error, which to the man on the job was of tiny consequence, in his chief's mind translated itself into losing a good customer—and losing thousands of good customers if the error should continue.

To the oil-house foreman or the bruise-trimmer's boss, my father doubtless seemed an unreasonable old gentleman who made a tremendous fuss about very little. On every subsequent visit to East St. Louis he lifted the sewer board of the oil-house cooler. Quite as unvaryingly on each inspection in Kansas City he stopped to watch the way the knife sliced out the bruises. Since he continued checking up on these operations several times a year for the rest of his life, to many of his people they doubtless seemed like hobbies of his.

Basically, of course, he comprehended a fundamental commercial truth: If everything is done right, if errors are held below the errors of competitors, and if a business serves an economic end, then it must prosper. He schooled himself to do everything absolutely right, and to expect the same of everyone else.

Perhaps the one point where he laid the most emphasis on having everything done absolutely right was in cleanliness. He insisted on cleanliness both because he liked it—it fitted in with his ideas of doing things right—and because it cut down spoilage materially.

The most noticeable improvement of the Chicago packing houses over the old local slaughterhouses was in cleanliness and sanitation. And father was the leader in this respect.

He had learned the lesson when he was a local retail dealer in meats back East. In those days when refrigeration was little employed, if at all, in the preservation of fresh meats, he had found out that meat which is handled fastidiously and kept in well-scrubbed containers does not spoil so quickly as when it is handled in slovenly fashion.

The principle, of course, is universal. There is less loss in handling steel or coal, just as with meat, if it is kept in a clean, orderly, well-planned way. In handling perishable foodstuffs this is outstandingly important.

But cleanliness cannot be obtained without eternal watchfulness. Dirt will accumulate if vigilance is relaxed. And the average human being seldom considers it worth while to keep up the fight.

Proof that it pays had come to him—rather he had worked it out—at Clinton, Massachusetts. After his original start with twenty-five dollars, nineteen of which bought a heifer and yielded a profit of ten dollars, he had scraped together a little capital for working funds—it was far from a fortune. It took him fourteen years from that start to save up enough money to carry out any plan at all extensive.

His first ambitious enterprise was opening a large retail meat market at Clinton. This was a move from sandy, sparse Cape Cod to the richer, more populous hinterland.

There were already here two or three small meat markets serving the local mill hands. They served, that is, by carrying a meagre stock of meats which they kept in their ice boxes—for by 1869 refrigeration was coming a little more generally into use. When a customer stated a desire for a given cut, the market man disappeared into the murky recesses and emerged either with a piece of meat from which he cut what was desired, or else with the information that he did not have the requested variety in stock.

There was no attractive display and no effort at cleanliness beyond what common sense dictated would save on meat spoilage. There was a deal of greasiness and little of daintiness.

My father, in his trips around New England buying and selling cattle, had done his best to sate his unquenchable inquisitiveness about anything bearing on the meat trade. He had consequently noticed that in the larger cities like Worcester and Providence and Boston the prosperous meat dealers were those who made their stores pleasant and their service nice.

So in his new Clinton market he put into effect all of his ideas which seemed practical from among those he had observed and he added a number of others he had never seen tried. Perhaps the larger cities had meat markets as attractive as his at Clinton. Certainly no other towns of that size had its equal, in quality or size.

To Swift's Market came wives of the hungry mill hands who made Bigelow Carpets and Lancaster

THE SLAUGHTERHOUSE AT BARNSTABLE. IN CIRCLE, THE WAGON THAT G. F. SWIFT DROVE WHEN HE SOLD HIS MEATS FROM DOOR TO DOOR.

Ginghams. They liked the cleanliness of the place—
the clean windows, the clean floors covered with
clean, fresh sawdust, the neatly scrubbed butcher
blocks and counters. They were a bit awed by the
white marble trays on which cuts of meat were displayed—but not too awed to buy the meat.

For the proprietor of this store deserved his reputation of being a finicky meat seller. He insisted
then, just as he insisted all of his life thereafter, that
"good enough" was never good enough. He wanted
everything right, every iota of it. If it was not, then
someone was in trouble.

The natives were not used to this nicety of handling meat, nor were they used to seeing cuts of meat
on display. Father displayed those cuts which he
most needed to dispose of. People who came in
bought them as a matter of course. And right here
is where he learned some of the fundamentals which
were to prove of utmost value in later years when
Swift's Market at Clinton was but a memory and
Swift & Company at Chicago was taking all of his
attention. The fundamentals of selling which he
had been developing in his earlier career and which
had been shaping themselves in his mind came into
their clear-cut shapes at Clinton. How he used them
to develop one of the world's largest businesses must
be reserved for a subsequent chapter.

From the store he had men operating three meat
wagons which daily sold over regular routes. His
own experience back on Cape Cod had included

driving a meat cart or two with himself as sole proprietor. Now, however, he was hiring others to do
this for him.

The carts were doing a business of perhaps twenty-
five dollars a day apiece. The market was doing
about fifty a day over the counter. And if you question whether thirty-five to forty thousand dollars a
year was a substantial volume for a small-town meat
dealer in those days, ask some old New England
housewife what her mother paid for meat about
1870. For fifteen cents a good-sized family could
have a meat meal; for twenty-five cents the table
could carry generous helpings of the choicest beef
ribs or loins.

Principally it was cleanliness and the will to do
things right which had made the Clinton market such
a success. These fundamentals are quite as important
today—more important, even—in any business which
deals with the general public. Standards have gone
up. The show market at Clinton would be an altogether ordinary market in any city of the same size
today. Any man who wants to stand out above competition must set new standards, just as my father set
new standards when he opened the Clinton market.

That is why he made a good profit regularly out of
the Clinton business. He always maintained that
if an operation was performed correctly, we made
money by it. Often after we had undertaken some
activity which lost money for us and kept on losing
money, he would say: "We lose because we haven't

learned yet how to do it. When we know how to do
it right, we'll begin to make it pay. But you can't
expect to make money when you do a thing wrong."

So he was always checking up, always looking for
things that were not being done exactly right. When
he inspected a plant—and this was frequent in his
routine—he would not let anyone go ahead of him.
He did not want it known that he was on the way.

He never looked at the big, showy things for
cleanliness. He looked in corners, down sewers,
under benches, and in the least well lighted parts
of coolers.

When he found something wrong, sarcasm was his
working tool for getting it corrected. "I think you
ought to hang an electric light on that so you could
see it," he told the foreman in charge of a beef cooler
when he found a long, heavy cobweb swinging down
from the ceiling.

"Do you think tallow's going down?" he inquired
of his brother Nat, in charge of the mutton cooler at
the Chicago wholesale market. Nat's frock was very
greasy.

"I don't know," responded Nathaniel.

"Well, I think it's going up. If I was you, I'd
fry out that frock right away. It's a chance to make
a good bit of money."

There was another time, when a new foreman could
not lay his hands on a clean white frock promptly
after word reached him by grapevine telegraph that
"G. F." was on the way. So he slipped out of his

dirty frock, and donned a new tan overcoat of fashionable cut.

"Do you work here?" was the first question.

"Yes, sir; I'm the foreman."

"I guess you didn't come down to stay all day," he commented.

The foreman needed no further hint. Off came his new coat. He went through the department without a frock. And today, risen to plant superintendent, he testifies that not since then has he ever mislaid his frock—nor ever worn a dirty one. That sort of thing, multiplied by thousands, is a contribution which father left us and which will never be outgrown. For the men he trained are training others in the same ways; and his lessons are thus passed on direct from one business generation to the next.

It was back before the days of concrete floors that he stopped, suspiciously eyed the planking, and asked the foreman of the killing floor at Kansas City: "How do you keep these floors clean?"

"We scrub them with soap every night, and once a week with sal soda," answered the foreman.

"We advertise cleanliness," observed his chief. "Use sal soda every night," he directed the plant superintendent who was going through with him. And the foreman, still active on a like job, remarks, "G. F. was the greatest man for sal soda ever I see!"

On this same killing floor, on the same visit, he called the foreman's attention to a negro cattle skinner who always put his foot on the inside of the hide. No one saw anything wrong with that. "Wait until they hoist the carcass," urged the president.

Sure enough, in the process the footprint from the inside of the hide—harmless enough in that place—"offset" onto the carcass when it was hoisted. It looked for all the world as if someone had been standing on the carcass. And it was not a sanitary practice.

No one had ever noticed this before, though the negro said he had been doing it ever since he came to work a year and a half before. Only a man with complete grasp of every detail of a complex business could have seen why this was bad practice. Father saw in passing what had escaped the men who spent full time right there. And with his passion for cleanliness and for having everything done shipshape, he corrected the situation at once.

One time back in the '90s while I was out of town, he took occasion every afternoon for weeks on end to call in a youngster who worked under me. Daily he lectured him about the crumbs of suet on the outside of carcasses dressed in this youngster's department. Finally the young man succeeded in getting everyone to brush off the crumbs of suet. It was years after the employee became manager of one of our largest plants that he discovered for himself why the old gentleman was so vehement about this. The broken tissues of the crumbs of suet allow mold spores to get a start, and thus to depreciate the carcass. G. F. Swift probably did not know this specifically. But he knew that anything perfectly clean and orderly kept longer than the same thing when mussy. The suet crumbs did not belong on the carcasses, hence he fussed about it until he got the beef coming through right.

In the early days he fired a floorsman at Chicago for having dirty arms—always a pet irritation to him. But this floorsman was a skilled workman. So the superintendent hired him back two years after, thinking that it had all been forgotten.

Three days afterwards father was going through the plant. "Isn't that the man I fired for dirty arms a year or so ago?"

"Yes, Mr. Swift."

"All right, fire him again. When I fire anybody, I want him to stay fired until I vote on him." Dirtiness around the plant was an unforgivable sin.

On every loading platform of our plants stood a tripe keg. The boy who swept off the platform had as part of his duty to pick up any fat which might fall off the carcasses and put it in the tripe keg before someone crushed it under foot. Never did father cross a shipping platform without looking up and down for these bits of crotch fat. If one was found flattened against the planking, the foreman and the boy both heard of it. For when this was overlooked, it crossed two of his prime ideas—it was dirty and it was wasteful. Either was a misdemeanor—the combination constituted a major crime.

Everything connected with the handling of his

goods was just right or else it was all wrong. He allowed no middle ground.

For example, he never failed to look over the beef coolers. It was part of his routine every time he visited a plant. He would don a frock and spend half an hour or so squinting down the long rows of beef carcasses. He paid particular attention to the neck fat and how it was trimmed. It must be trimmed to exactly the right conformation to look pleasing, but there must not be a hair's breadth extra trimmed off. Fat on the carcass was worth the carcass or quarter price. Trimmed off, it was tankage, or, at best, oleo oil.

If he saw a carcass which looked wrong somehow as he squinted down the long row, he would examine it closely. If he saw a dark spot on the sawdust covering of the floor, there was bound to be trouble. Things must be clean; things must be done right. Anything else called for a reprimand.

When it came to the cuts, his inspection was likewise of the closest. Beef ribs are very desirable and bring a high price. Chuck is not so highly thought of by the American housewife and therefore is less in demand. When a carcass is cut absolutely right, it yields nine per cent rib and twenty-six per cent chuck. If the cut is made at the wrong place, the carcass will yield perhaps eight per cent rib and twenty-seven per cent chuck. He never lost an opportunity to point out to a foreman what it cost to do this wrong.

For father was a teacher, along with his insistence on doing everything right. I remember when I was nine or ten years old, back in Massachusetts, how he used to get me up sometimes before daylight to help him butcher a steer. My part was to hold the lantern.

Boylike, I would become so interested in some side line of activity that I would forget my part of the job. He never used to lose his temper, even though the lantern would go into eclipse just at the moment when he most needed its light. Instead he would say: "You'll want to know some day how to do what I'm doing now. Hold the lantern so that you can see. Then I can see, too."

He knew how to buy cattle and how to pick cattle buyers. He knew that the only way to buy cattle was by the most painstaking care and that the only way to check up on the results was to look over the cattle as they came to the skinning floor.

When father first came to Chicago, everyone used to laugh at his habit of riding a low Texas pony which left his legs dangling almost to the ground. He would ride around on his low-slung steed buying his cattle and caring little what anyone else might think. He knew why he was doing it and he knew he was right.

In the first place, he could let himself into a cattle pen without bothering to get off his horse—or without taking a boy around with him to do this job. But more important still, he was down at about the level of the cattle's backs. He could reach over and feel the butts of the cattle to see whether there was any fat there. A great many wise jokes were made about this habit of his.

Finally, however, someone inquired just why he felt the rump of every beef animal he bought. "Back where I ship these cattle to, they're bought that way. That's how I sell 'em, and how I buy 'em." He was simply applying at Chicago the test which he knew each animal would have to meet when it reached Brighton or Albany. And when his cattle brought a better price in those markets than did other shippers' cattle, this was the reason. He always tried to find out the right way to do a thing, and then he followed out this right procedure unfailingly.

There were dozens, yes hundreds, of points which he had settled as the best way of doing a thing, and on which he checked up by personal observation at every opportunity. Sometimes he could not demonstrate the right way. Nevertheless he knew what the wrong way was and what the right.

He stopped one day in the Chicago packing house to show one of his old-time New England butchers how to split a bullock. It was years since he had personally wielded a cleaver and his hand had lost its cunning. He did it clumsily and made a poor job of it. "Now, then, that's not how to do it," he explained to the old-timer, "but you know how it should be done. Do it the right way. If a thing's worth doing at all, it's worth doing right."

If a thing's worth doing at all, it's worth doing right. This was father's creed and pretty nearly the whole set of rules he ran by. He repeated that copy-book maxim thousands of times, to thousands of different people who worked for him. And he said it each time with the simple faith and conviction which made the other man appreciate the basic truth in the hackneyed words.

Every detail of the business was at his finger tips. He knew cattle-dressing, for example, as well as any one I have ever encountered. He insisted on prompt sticking to prevent dark meat. He always looked into the carcass to see that no skirt meat had been cut away with the viscera—for it is easy to lose a quarter-pound of meat per animal in this way, which really means something in the course of a day.

At St. Joseph a new method had been devised for performing an operation in splitting a hog—it consisted of using shears instead of a knife to split the aitch-bone, and is nowadays standard procedure. But at that time it had just been devised and was to be tested out at Chicago in my father's presence.

So at the appointed time he walked to the spot in the plant where the test was to be conducted. The hogs were in improper shape. Someone had scalded them and had left the hair on. Without a word he picked up a knife and began taking off the hair. Everybody else turned to and inside a few minutes the hogs were scraped.

Then he walked back to the place where he could

see best and the others prepared for the test. The plant functionaries were all there. They showed him the new operation, explained to him its advantages, and awaited his verdict.

Not a word had he said from the time he saw the hogs hanging there. He had simply worked and listened.

Now when the others had finished talking and hung on his decision as to whether the new method should be considered standard henceforth, he said, to their surprise:

"You know, when you're dressing hogs you ought to take the hair off; you ought, ought to take the hair off. Never ought to leave a hog like that." And he walked back to his office without a word about the new method of cutting the aitch-bone.

He was much more concerned about maintaining a right method than about adopting a new method. Therein he showed that common sense which distinguished his ways of working from those of so many men of greater apparent brilliance. Once he had a good method established he never allowed anyone, himself included, to overlook it. He was ready to supplant it at any time if a better method came his way. But he avoided that common failing of being so busy with new-hatched plans that he overlooked the old, tested, profitable methods.

His everlasting desire that things be done right was in no sense confined to his business. He felt exactly the same way in everything he came in contact with and used to go out of his way to see that things were done as they should be.

Father was not at all averse to doing them, if need be. He went to church regularly. I do not believe that he ever arose less than half a dozen times during a service to raise or lower a window or two. He wanted the ventilation of the church just right, just as he wanted every one of his refrigerator cars scrubbed out and cleaned with live steam between trips. It was not that he wanted to be officious— though I dare say a good many people thought him so in this respect. Rather it was his desire that the ventilation be right. Since the church could employ no corps of workmen to do the job, he was willing to do it himself.

He was always inveighing against a style which was current for several years of wearing black hats in the summer time. "You ought not to wear a black hat in the summer," he would tell his employees— or a caller from outside, perhaps someone he had never seen before that day. "Black draws the sun. You ought to wear a light hat." Again, it was not his desire to be meddlesome but rather his feeling that everything ought to be absolutely right all of the time. If it was not, if he saw anything which was not as it should be, it made him so uncomfortable that he tried to set it right.

At Omaha those men who drove their own horses to work (this was in the late '90s) maintained a horse shed with a boy in charge of their horses. My father's natural inquisitiveness led him thither one day and he did not think that everything was as it should be. "Your horses aren't looking very good. Better give 'em a bran mash once in a while," he directed.

It was almost a year later that he made his next visit to the Omaha plant. As soon as he was through in the office and on the plant he headed for the horse shed. The same boy was on the job. "Your horses look better than last time I saw them," was his comment. "Guess those bran mashes helped 'em along." He had trained himself never to forget anything until he had seen it to a successful conclusion. Even when he was running one of the world's largest businesses he could not overlook the condition of the horses he had noticed a year before.

It was the same way whether he was checking up on the loss of horse blankets at one of the Chicago wholesale markets or making sure that the standard shade of paint was being used on all Swift properties. In both instances he was interested in having things exactly right and also in saving money. But he was even more concerned with the rightness than he was with the saving.

In overseas selling, especially in England, he ran into trade abuses which could not be tolerated by his standards. He made, altogether, more than twenty trips across to get them cleared up.

When he started at it, American-dressed meats had no show to be sold either attractively or economically.

Before he had finished with the job, American meats were going to Great Britain by the shipload and he was realizing the real value of his products. Moreover, a great deal more of his beef was being sold there than of locally raised beef.

He used to get up at three o'clock every morning in London to go over into Smithfield Market and check up on what was being done with his product. He would row with any marketman who tried to perpetuate a trade abuse. And eventually he cleaned the situation up. He was quite as interested in accomplishing this because it was right as because it gave him another profitable market—though he did not discount the market, at that.

Father's knowledge of every part of the business and his attention to the most minute details was one of the secrets of his operating success. While the microscopic eye was his for scrutinizing little things, he had the telescopic eye for surveying big things. And he never put on the wrong lens!

CHAPTER IV

TAKING THE EAST

YOU never made any money on business you
didn't do."

This was the idea which governed my father's
whole activity. If you did a good job of selling, you
had a chance to make money—you *made* money,
assuming your business was competently managed.
But if you did not sell, then you stood no chance to
make it.

"You don't make a profit on shortages," was
another of his maxims. Every morning he carefully
looked over the previous day's orders which could
not be filled completely because we hadn't the goods
in stock to ship.

I still follow this custom. Shortages may readily
cut two per cent or even more off the total sales. And
when we are working every day to build up our volume at a profit, I see little sense in throwing away
trade.

As long as a manager sold plenty, G. F. Swift stood
by him—even if he made no money. Failure to make
money on a big enough trade simply showed that a
condition existed which could with thought be corrected.

But failure to sell put the man in a hole. If he did

65

not sell when his job was selling, then someone soon replaced him.

Whenever he faced the job of breaking in where he had had no trade, father was a plunger. He would quickly take a chance to lose a lot of money if that was the key to getting a big trade quickly.

When he decided to sell Chicago-dressed beef in New York City, he hired a man there—and forthwith shipped him a car of beef, followed by another a week later. Then in a few days he went to New York.

"How are you making out?" was the first question he shot at the salesman.

"Awfully bad, Mr. Swift. I lost you a thousand dollars on each of those two cars."

In these early days two thousand dollars was a whole lot of money to father. But he never blinked an eye. "All right. You'll do better next week, won't you?"

"I hope so, Mr. Swift. I hate to promise." The salesman was a conscientious, hard-working fellow.

"Well, I'm going to ship you three cars next week. Sell it somehow."

With the knowledge that he could count on a boss determined to sell beef in New York regardless, the man succeeded in disposing of those three cars at a smaller loss than his previous record. The week after, he just about broke even.

Very soon he was making a little money on each car he handled; he was handling a goodly number of cars each week. His trade grew so that it wiped out the red-ink figures within a few weeks more. In less than six months we were an important factor in the New York market—at a profit.

"If you're going to lose money, lose it. But don't let 'em nose you out." This was my father's standard policy and his standard advice: to the pioneer New York man; to the man in charge of our British beef business; to his brother Edwin, who handled the eastern sales after a few years; to me when I was starting the pork and provision ends of the business a few years later.

"Don't let 'em nose you out." It is about as good advice as can be given to any man anywhere.

After the first two or three cars of Chicago-dressed beef had been quickly and profitably sold in Lowell, Massachusetts, the local market men agreed to buy no more Swift beef—and bound their bargain by posting cash forfeits. So the next car we shipped ran against a figurative stone wall.

The evening of the first day a telegram came from the Lowell agent: "Local butchers combined agreeing buy no Chicago beef. No sale for beef in Lowell. Shall I ship the car to Lawrence or where?"

"Sell it in Lowell," his chief wired laconically.

Next evening came another telegram: "No sales today. Where shall I sell it?"

Again the answer: "Sell it in Lowell."

The Lowell experience was by no means unique. Our agents in the East were having none too easy a time of it in many instances. They met with opposition, frequently well-organized opposition.

Nearly every agent was applying from time to time for permission to ship his beef elsewhere. Chicago-dressed beef was never going to be established anywhere if the agents were allowed to give up. My father put a stop to it, nor permitted any exceptions.

Next day anyone in Lowell could buy Swift beef at the price he offered. That day the car was sold out.

Within less than a week the chief arrived in Lowell. In rapid succession he bought a lot, obtained a switch track, and had lumber delivered to the site. Next day a branch-house market was being erected.

Before the market was opened, one of the outstanding local dealers called on him. "I was in the combination against you," the native began. "But I'd like to handle Swift beef as your local agent."

"We lost five hundred dollars on a car of beef because of your boycott," he was told. "If you assume that loss, I'll be glad to have you as my partner in this market." The deal was closed right then. G. F. Swift would not be nosed out, but he thought no less of the man who tried it.

That was typical—except for the boycott—of how he broke into many an eastern town. Usually he began by having his beef sold out of the car, or from the platform on a switch track. Then, if he could, he would get local wholesale dealers to handle the beef. Sometimes he had to put in salaried men because he could not find the sort of local dealer to whom he would entrust the job.

When Chicago-dressed beef began coming on the market, the East had a real prejudice against it. To be sure, it had better edible qualities, by reason of hanging in refrigeration for several days after slaughter, than had the fresh-killed beef the easterners had been eating.

But the idea of eating meat a week or more after it had been killed met with a nasty-nice horror. There was about as much sense in avoiding Chicago-dressed beef as there would have been if the reformers a few years before had succeeded in doing away with sanitary plumbing in residences. Each was a marked improvement over the old order. Yet each was guilty of the original sin of newness.

While he had hard situations to meet in some places, in many others he was able to get the most desirable agents merely for the asking. His reputation as a business man and as a meat man was enviable throughout New England. Even though he had been away several years, his reputation held its old gleam. G. F. Swift's word that his product was good and marketable was enough for most of his friends.

He always went to the best possible local man. If this man could not be obtained as agent, then an employee got the job.

"There's no use handling poor stuff or dealing with the wrong sort of people," father used to explain. "There are enough people who want good stuff and who will deal honestly, to give us all the business we can handle." This was his guiding principle in picking men or live stock.

He simply wore off the prejudice against western beef—where he could, by diplomacy. Where diplomacy proved inadequate, he resorted to open warfare.

In Fitchburg, for example, Lowe & Sons was the leading firm of meat dealers. As soon as he was able to furnish Chicago-dressed beef in winter—this was eighteen months before the first successful warm-weather shipment was delivered at Fall River—father called on the elder Lowe.

Lowe not only refused the agency, he was downright unpleasant about it. "I wouldn't sell a pound of your beef if Fitchburg was starving," he vehemently declared.

"All right, I'll feed Fitchburg myself," was the retort.

So my eldest uncle, William Swift, went to Fitchburg as our agent. "G. F." was a natural trader; but William had trading, old-fashioned Yankee trading, down to a fine art. His original keenness in this direction had been sharpened up by infinite practice and observation. He would swap horses or jack-knives—and never to my knowledge did he get the worse of a trade.

If a market man would let William Swift supply a quarter or a side or a carcass of western beef, he would trade for a calf or a sheep or a barrel of pork—then sell the swapped stuff for cash. If a customer who had bought on credit showed signs of weakening, he would back up a wagon and load up enough pork or any other portable assets there might be to square accounts.

William Swift supplied competition which was real competition. He cleaned up the local business at a profit, nor left much for the Lowes. It was not long before the old established firm of Lowe & Sons had retired from business, leaving the field pretty much to Swift beef.

But here, once more, father joined forces with the enemy after the defeat. Three of the Lowe boys came to Chicago and went to work for him. After a few years they went back home to Fitchburg and started in again, handling Swift products exclusively. Until about fifty years after the historic encounter between G. F. Swift and the elder Lowe, a Lowe was managing Swift & Company's Fitchburg branch house.

G. F. Swift when he was going after trade would always give a competitor a chance to join with him. "If you'll handle my beef, we'll be partners. If you won't handle my beef, I'll put it in against you." This was the squarest kind of competition. And if it came to competition, my father always won. He had the mighty advantage of economics on his side.

Beyond even his ability as a packer was his ability as a trader. He was, to be sure, a superlative manufacturer in his chosen field. But it was as a trader that he excelled.

"The best cattle always sell first," was one of his

maxims. Another was, "Sell off the odds and ends
first. You can always sell the top pieces."

He believed a good man sold what was hard to sell.
He emphasized on every occasion that anyone can sell
beef tenderloins and rib roasts if his customer has the
money—but it takes real ability to sell a chuck pot-
roast to a customer who wants to buy porterhouse
steak. "See that row of houses over there?" he
inquired of one of his managers with whom he was
in 1900 revisiting Sandwich, the Cape Cod home
town of his youth. "That's where I used to peddle
meat. Many a time the women came out of those
houses to buy—and usually I sold 'em what I had the
most of," he ended with a chuckle.

When Texas longhorns were coming into the stockyards in quantity, they were not in high esteem.
Texas beef was not the most easily salable. Yet we of
course slaughtered our share.

My father visited the Cleveland branch house once
and saw perhaps two hundred Texas cattle in the
cooler. "You needn't say a word about those cattle,"
he told the manager. "I can tell all about 'em.
They're on your mind, aren't they?"

"You bet they are."

"If I had those cattle on my mind, I wouldn't have
'em there by tonight. I'd have 'em on somebody else's
mind by tonight."

"I'd have to sell them at a ridiculous price, Mr.
Swift."

"I'd have 'em off *my* mind."

LONGHORNS CAME FROM THE PLAINS OF TEXAS.

Next day he wired from Buffalo: "How many of those cattle are left?"

"No cattle left," the Cleveland manager telegraphed back. His men were seldom slow to take his hints.

G. F. Swift never believed in holding to a thing because selling it might bring a loss. For one thing, fresh meat is perishable. And again, he believed that the best way to make money is to keep turning over goods and capital. He developed a technique which kept his goods moving at a rate far faster than was needed to avoid spoilage. I doubt whether he could have built up his tremendous business in so short a time otherwise. As it was, he was kept scratching for funds to run his business. Because he made every dollar do the work of ten, he expanded much faster than he otherwise could have.

Yet with all of his desire to sell and then sell some more, he kept warning his people not to overload a customer: "Never try to sell a customer more of anything than he can get rid of quickly. Try to sell him what he needs, and then he'll come back. He'll be a better customer in the end."

Similarly he held that smaller customers should not be discriminated against in price. "It isn't wise to make extra low prices to big customers on large quantities," was the way he told it. "Encourage the small customer. Maybe some day he'll be a big customer."

And when he made a price, it stuck. Whether he was selling or buying, he stood by his price.

It was based on worth as he saw it. Father would not change his price unless conditions changed. And often it angered him to have someone come back to him with another offer.

One of his fundamentals of selling he proved out in his retail market at Clinton, back before he came to Chicago. He had driven a retail cart on Cape Cod, selling to housewives meat which he had slaughtered. Then he had come to Brighton market, near Boston, to buy his cattle and drive them to Barnstable for slaughtering. Next he devised the plan of doing his slaughtering at Brighton, selling the meat along the way as he drove home to Barnstable.

He saw the chance to branch out as a cattle buyer. He would buy cattle from the farmers who raised a cow or two for market, drive them to Brighton, and sell them there.

By the time he had developed through fourteen or fifteen years of these varying but related experiences, he opened his market at Clinton. The success of this market has already been described, but one phase of it deserves more than casual attention. For one of the methods he devised there to sell meat to housewives who entered the shop was carried over into selling meat at wholesale when we had wholesale markets stretched from coast to coast.

The meat-market men who had the Clinton trade before father opened his store there used to keep their meat in the ice box. Nothing was on display.

Father had learned, years before, that he had to sell

off the plate and chuck and round if he was to make his profits from the animal. And he had developed the knack of convincing his retail customers that these were the parts they should buy—if at the time it was the sort of meat he had the most of. He knew that the ribs and loins take care of selling themselves.

So when he opened his Clinton market he displayed tempting cuts of meat where customers could not fail to see them. His store was clean in every detail, no one could take exception to having the meats outside the cooler.

He made a point of displaying most prominently those cuts which he needed to sell. The sirloin-steak customer could be depended upon to insist on getting sirloin steak. But a woman who came in undecided, and whose pocketbook was thin, would profit both herself and the store by buying one of the less popular cuts.

The plan worked—worked beautifully. Not only did customers buy the meat he wanted to sell, but also six times out of ten they bought more than they had intended buying. It was exactly the principle of store display which has subsequently been employed by progressive retail merchants. The five- and ten-cent store chains are the prominent examples of using this plan. Store display is the mainspring of their success.

In pursuing his idea of store display, father discovered that if you cut them up, you sell more cattle in a day. (The same thing applies, of course, to

every other kind of animal. But in the early days at
Chicago he dealt only in beef. Mutton and pork
came later.)

When a retail meat dealer enters our wholesale
market to buy something, he is probably aware that
he has a good-sized stock of meats in his ice box. If
he sees in the wholesale cooler row upon row of
whole carcasses, or even of quarters, he simply
remembers the general condition of his stock and
buys nothing beyond what he came in to get.

But if he sees instead a large assortment of cuts in
the foreground, with the larger pieces in the background, he begins to particularize in his mind. "I've
got too many rounds left," he may think. "But I'm
getting pretty low on ribs. Better buy some, so I
won't be running out." We make the additional sale,
which likewise helps him to keep his stock better bal-
anced and his customers satisfied because they find at
his store exactly what they want.

"Cut it up and scatter the pieces," the chief would
direct the manager of a branch house where a cooler
of beef was not moving well. "The more you cut, the
more you sell." The advantage of the small sale now
instead of the large sale later is obvious. And there is
the benefit to the dealer who is better able to turn his
stock when he buys cuts instead of quarters. "If they
won't buy a whole carcass," father would tell a man
whose sales were slow, "maybe they'll buy a cut."

Inertia militates against doing things this way. It
is hard work to cut up beef carcasses into cuts for

display. The unambitious manager hated to go to all this trouble. But after his chief had jumped him for it a few times and he had seen for himself how rapidly meat sold in cuts when the carcasses from which the cuts came had not been selling, even the laziest manager learned the wisdom of the plan.

Once father dropped in to see a man who had recently left us to take charge of another packer's St. Louis wholesale market. There was a big selection of cuts on hand in the cooler, well displayed and thoroughly attractive.

"Nice lot of cuts you've got here, Halloway," commented his former boss. "Don't know when I've ever seen a better line of cuts in a cooler."

"I don't think you ever did, Mr. Swift," replied Halloway. "But it's your idea, and it's doing just what you always said it would. You told me once, years ago, that you literally cut your way into the beef business any place you opened a market. I'm trying to cut my way into it for these people here in St. Louis. You taught me that, Mr. Swift. And I'll tell you, we're cutting our way in."

"Cut it up and scatter it out." This was one of the principles which made sales for my father and which worked quite as well for him in other lines of activity. I have already told how he placed Swift financial paper in the hands of every small bank which wanted it. This was an application of the same theory, one of the best ideas which was ever devised in our financing. The country banks got accustomed to having Swift paper, in small pieces. They learned it was safe stuff to have, and when a pinch came they held to it as if it were government bonds.

His financial policies and his sales policies touched in at least one other important point. He intermeshed so completely the financial interests of many important distributors with the interests of Swift & Company that there was no question that we had adequate, enthusiastic sales representation.

His chief assistance in this whole field of developing and insuring thorough distribution was his brother Edwin C. Swift. "E. C." was ten years younger and had been father's first lieutenant before father came to Chicago. He had managed the Clinton retail market after his elder brother's interests had ramified, when the larger affairs of Hathaway & Swift, and Anthony, Swift & Company, were claiming G. F. Swift's attention. After the Clinton retail market was sold, E. C. continued to run the wholesale business at Clinton.

But when G. F. Swift's whole interest was transferred to the Chicago business and its development through the early stages of slaughtering in the West and shipping to the East, E. C. and he had parted. E. C. wanted to see the country. He had gone to the Pacific Coast, and what had become of him there no one in the family knew. Letters sent to his last address at San Francisco came back unclaimed.

Once the technical problems of the young enterprise had been met at Chicago, there came the need

EDWIN C. SWIFT

D. M. ANTHONY

for developing eastern trade just as fast as was humanly possible. Father could not carry the whole load; he could not be both in Chicago running his company and in New England building up its trade. He spent as much time in the East as he could, but it was not enough, and he knew it.

So he naturally thought of his brother Edwin. Edwin knew father's ways of working, was trustworthy and energetic, was a good mixer. In short, Edwin was exactly the man to take charge of eastern affairs.

But where was E. C.? No one knew. G. F. determined to find him, for he never let any ordinary difficulties stop him.

So he sent for a relative who was working at Chicago and who knew Edwin well. He gave him a comparatively large sum of money and directed: "I want you to find Edwin. Here is the last address we had for him, in San Francisco. You'll have to trace him from there. But you must find him. And when you find him, bring him to me at once. I must have him come here to see me."

After a good deal of amateur detective work in San Francisco, the relative found Edwin C. Swift's name on the pay roll of a railroad contractor. The gang was engineering a railroad eastward across the mountains, several hundred miles from San Francisco. The messenger set out to find the gang, and succeeded after several weeks of hard travel.

"What does Stave want of me?" was the first

question Edwin asked after the messenger had told
him he was wanted.

"I don't know, Bub. But I know he told me to
bring you without fail, that he had to see you in
Chicago. You know he wouldn't have gone to all
this length to hunt you up if he hadn't meant it."

"But I'm bound here by a contract," protested
E. C. "I can't leave this job. And I like it here,
anyhow."

The messenger stuck to it. He kept after E. C.
for two weeks or so, and finally persuaded him to
make the change. It took a while longer to find
a man to replace him, but eventually they started
eastward. Sharing one horse to Ogden, two hundred
miles away from their start, they there boarded a
train and came to Chicago in comparative comfort.

When the brothers had talked, E. C. saw that the
opportunity in the East was just his sort of job. So
he took it on and became a partner. He was then
twenty-nine, my father thirty-nine. Between them
they developed trade at a rate which actually surprised them both.

When E. C. Swift joined us at this time the parent
concern was known as G. F. Swift & Company. In
the East it was selling as Swift Brothers. And it
was not so long afterwards that the whole business
was incorporated as Swift & Company, with three
hundred thousand dollars capital stock—in less than
two years to be increased to three millions.

Father had personally gone into partnership with

many of the eastern dealers who became his local agents. He and Edwin C. Swift sold a good deal of the stock to many of the eastern dealers who became his local agents, key men in the East. Thus with part of the agency owned by G. F. Swift and with the more important agents heavy stockholders in the company, there were built up outlets which gave unquestioned loyalty and enthusiasm.

This solidarity of interest meant that our sales went up at an almost unbelievable rate. The important men at the yards had not believed it possible for father to succeed in dressing his meat at Chicago and selling it in the great consuming centers. They had been content to go ahead with their own affairs of smoking and salting pork, or of selling dressed beef locally around Chicago.

While they were waiting for their Yankee competition to fail, G. F. and E. C. built up a fresh meat business such as no one had ever dreamed of. The brothers put their whole minds, hearts, and strength into its development. By the time the other packers realized what was taking place, our slaughtering and shipping fresh beef and mutton had reached a point which gave us a tremendous lead. In this chosen field, the others could never catch up.

CHAPTER V

MANY A MINUTE . . . .

BY HIS last-minute, hair-breadth methods of doing, he saved more time than most men have altogether." This statement was made by a man who worked closely with my father for a long term of years.

It brings out, as well as can be brought out, one of his personal working methods which accounts for a great share of what G. F. Swift accomplished. It was largely through applying his energies without a waste motion or minute that he built up a large and profitable business in a comparatively short time.

I have known rather closely a good many business men who have made large successes. Most of them have been personally efficient.

They have applied their energies in ways that brought large results.

But I have yet to see anyone whose methods of working could compare with my father's. He made every minute, every idea count. He centered his thought and his time on his work. Swift & Company was the almost inevitable result.

Not a business man of his day or this day but could profit by adopting bodily many of G. F. Swift's working methods. They were sound and fundamentally simple. Literally, he saved more time than any other man I have ever known.

Out of this characteristic has grown a whole fund of stories—most of them true—about how he saved a minute here and five minutes there. Any old-timer in the Chicago stockyards can reel them off and can usually testify that he personally witnessed part of them.

Every Swift employee during G. F. Swift's lifetime knew, for instance, that if he ever saw the chief's horse and buggy pulled up at a railroad crossing, deserted, it was his duty to get in and drive to the barn with it. And almost every employee whose duties took him outside performed this task on one occasion or another.

The reason was that thus the boss saved time. Then, as now, long freight trains poked through the yards—and showed that perverse tendency of freight trains to stop on crossings. When a freight train halted G. F. Swift at a crossing, he looked to see whether the caboose was about to pass. If it was not, and he was near where he was going, out he jumped, climbed through the freight train, and left his horse beside the track to be put away by the first of his employees who happened along.

If, on the other hand, he was a long way from his destination and a long train was passing, he sometimes managed to signal the engineer to stop the train. He would step between the cars on the crossing, uncouple them and signal the engineer to pull up a few

feet. Then he would drive through, couple up the
train again, and be on his way. He would spend a
minute or two at hard work any time in order to save
a five-minute wait.

He never started for a destination until the elev-
enth hour. But he always got there on time. His
chases after the "dummy," the train which used to
be the only fast transportation between the Yards
and the Loop, have yielded a crop of stories which
might make a minor epic.

One man tells of an occasion when G. F. summoned him to Chicago from a Missouri city. Their
talk was to start on the train which father had to
take to a downtown meeting. And the visitor occu-
pied a chair in the private office until they should
be ready to start.

At ten minutes before train time the man from
the information desk walked into the office and said,
"Dummy leaves in ten minutes, Mr. Swift." There
was no sign from the busy man at the desk. In one
minute the clerk entered and said, "Only nine minutes now for the dummy." Thereafter he entered
every minute with his reminder. Finally he said,
"Only four minutes now, Mr. Swift. You'll miss
the dummy."

"I'll miss no dummy," retorted his chief, leaping
into action. With two or three motions he had gathered up his hat, his coat, the papers he needed.
"Come on," he shouted to the astonished visitor—and
down the stairs they fled three steps at a time. The

buggy was waiting at the door, with a boy holding
the horse's bridle.   As G. F. Swift came out the
door the horse, experienced at these affairs, started
off at a run with the two men swinging into their
seats as best they could.

"I never want such a wild ride again," declares
the man who was the unwilling participant.   "We
went through all that traffic without even slowing
up.   Mr. Swift never picked up the reins, just left
them on the dash.   As we swung up to the station,
the conductor was starting the train.   'Come on,'
Mr. Swift cried, and jumped to the ground before
the horse had even slowed up.   I scrambled after,
and somehow we managed to catch the train which
by this time was a few yards down the track.   'Well,
I didn't miss the dummy, did I?' the chief remarked
triumphantly, and we settled down to our business.
With him it was apparently all in the day's work."

On one such occasion the horse swung the buggy
into a telegraph pole and wrecked it.   Father had
a dozen close shaves in his wild rides to catch the
dummy.   Yet he never missed it.   And since he did
not allow himself to become in the least ruffled by
his hurry, he lost nothing to offset the time that he
saved in this way.

When he went to catch a street car, his driver was
never allowed to stop for the first car.   Instead, the
horse was speeded up and the next street car ahead
overtaken.   Then the car was stopped and the pas-
senger got aboard—one car ahead of where he would

have been if he had followed the conventional practice.

His time saving was not always spectacular, but it was always at work. He never used two minutes for any job if one would suffice. He never idled away the minute he had saved. In handling mail, for instance, he plowed through prodigious quantities by methods which would serve as well for almost any man in a position where he could plan his own office arrangements.

He was the best correspondent in our offices. His letters said everything that needed to be said on the subject at hand. Yet they contained never a useless phrase. And particularly if they were concerned with other than business affairs, as some of them must inevitably be, he cut off all the fringe and trimmings. He went terribly to the point.

I recall a letter written him by a friend who took perhaps a page and a half to weigh the pros and cons of the candidates in the pending presidential election. He ended by asking father's opinion as to who would be elected. The answer has stuck in my mind as a masterpiece of brevity in letter writing. It went:

"I am guessing that Mr. McKinley will be elected. You have the same privilege."

Time was the great element in his life. There was nowhere near enough of it to let him do all the things he wanted to do. He had no patience with anyone or anything which wasted time, his time in particular. His files, for example, had to be in charge of a mature man. It was no job for an office boy in those days when boys commonly handled files. His files had to give up to him anything he wanted, and at once. Let thirty seconds elapse between the time he called for a letter or document and the time it was placed on his desk—someone heard from it, heard from it strongly enough so that the crime was not repeated.

This was not captiousness. It was common sense. He had no overdeveloped sense of personal dignity. He required no kow-towing. But when he wanted something he wanted it without wasting any of the fleeting minutes of his busy day.

He wrote his letters on a half sheet of paper. He wanted others to be as considerate in writing to him. He abhorred receiving long letters. Going through his morning mail he would come to a long letter. Some few of his managers used to write voluminous letters, despite his best efforts to break them of the habit. "What does it say, what does it say?" he would demand impatiently, tossing the letter to his secretary. The secretary as a regular part of his duties boiled down long letters and returned them to his chief with a one- or two-paragraph summary. Father never read the original unless the summary indicated some point on which he wanted the fullest information.

He did not care about having things fixed up to look nice at the expense of his time. Once, at the height of his money troubles of 1893, he called for

a list of the notes outstanding. He wanted it right
away and could do nothing until he had it. So he
stood watching the employee who was making out
the list. Halfway through, a credit slip was placed
on the clerk's desk as notification that one of the
notes had been paid. It happened to be a note which
had already been listed. So the clerk got out an
eraser and began to correct the report.

"Put down the net, put down the net," father
almost shouted when he saw what the clerk was
doing. "I want the net, I don't want it pretty." He
heartily disliked any duplication of work for appearances' sake.

Certainly he was right about it. Time is one asset
which cannot be increased. And most of us waste
tremendous quantities of it without getting a com-
mensurate return. Nearly every business man devotes an inordinate amount of time to "keeping up
appearances" and to idle talk which has no reason
for taking up his minutes. The man who puts to
one side all of the useless frills of the business day
and keeps himself to the essential affairs quickly finds
he has performed in one day not only that day's work
but also a lot of back work which he has been intending for weeks to get at, but "hasn't had time for."
The time is there, but we waste it.

"When I realize the proportion of my time that
I used to waste, it makes me feel as though I have
misspent half my life," an acquaintance told me not
long ago. He has in the course of twenty years or

so built up one of the great manufacturing companies of the country. But he declares regretfully, "If I hadn't wasted time so lavishly all my life—excepting only the years when I was getting this business of mine started—I'd have had it ten years further along than it is right now." His situation differs from most men's only in that he recognizes his loss.

Using time to good advantage involves principally setting standards of what is worth taking time for and what is not—then holding up these self-imposed regulations. G. F. Swift believed that he did his best work only when he had had adequate sleep. So he left word, once the worst times of stress in the business were past, that he must not be awakened at night for any calls whatever.

A friend tells a story that one night continued telephone ringing awakened a servant. After she heard the message, she rapped on father's door until he responded. "They want to tell you that your packing house is burning down," the maid said.

"Tell them they can tell me about it at seven o'clock in the morning," was his reply, and back he went to sleep. He knew that nothing he could do would impede the fire. If it really was a serious fire, it might take serious planning next morning to meet the emergency. Very well. He would be in better condition to meet the emergency after a good night's sleep. So he got the sleep.

Another time, lightning struck the barn back of the house and it began to burn brightly. This was perhaps at ten o'clock, just before he was ready to go to bed. The barn was not far from his bedroom window.

With his superintendent, who lived down the street a way, he stood in the street and watched the firemen at work. They had the fire stopped, it was making no progress. He yawned, looked at his watch, and turned to the superintendent. "It's half past ten and I guess I'll go to bed," he remarked. "You and the firemen can get that fire put out, Foster. There's no reason why I should stay up." And with the flames still crackling, he went to bed and to sleep at once.

He was all for business all of the time. He kept long hours when there was occasion for them. In the early days when it was a struggle to make expenses and income balance he left the house at five o'clock every morning for the stockyards. At that time he bought all of the cattle we handled. He didn't need any help, nor could he afford the expense of hiring a cattle buyer. By the time he had to spend his full time in the office and the packing house, he had trained me into the cattle buying. For some time I did all of it. Then as I went on to other duties my five brothers followed me. It was some time before finally he brought on Wellington Leavitt from Brighton to be our head cattle buyer. By then the business had expanded to many times its original size.

Even after the business was well established and making good profits father did not altogether give

LOUIS F. SWIFT

up his early morning habits. We had a good deal
of trouble with the treatment accorded our products
by the English butchers during the first few years
we were in the British markets. He made several
trips to England to correct this difficulty.

During all of his time in London, three o'clock
every morning saw him at Smithfield Market, the
focus of the troubles. The rest of the day, after the
Smithfield business was done, by nine or ten o'clock,
he devoted to the more routine matters of our British
agencies. His efforts cleared up a bad situation
which might never have been cleared up without his
early rising.

It was not only early in the morning but also late
in the evening when we were getting a start in Chicago. He was not alone in this, the whole family
worked with him. Mother was for many years the
only bookkeeper he had. He and she used every
night to make out the beef sheets, the shipping directions for next day's work. A little later the boys
had the same job. The whole family, or that part
of it which was sufficiently grown up to do so, worked
every evening until ten or eleven o'clock.

"What time is it, Mr. Swift?" a workman inquired of him as he strode through a workroom in
the days when a hundred men or so constituted the
whole force.

"You'll know when the whistle blows!" snapped
the boss, always in a hurry and in no temper to waste
time to relieve a clock watcher's mind.

"When a clerk says he must leave the office because it is five o'clock, you'll never see his name over a front door," he has been quoted as saying. No wonder he had so little patience with the clock watcher.

His own life had shown him how necessary is hard work in getting a start. If it had not been for the terrific hours he put in, I doubt whether G. F. Swift could ever have got the start he did. He came to Chicago with thirty thousand dollars, which even then was altogether inadequate as capital for the smallest packing business. And broad as had been his experience in every side of the live-stock and meat business, he lacked first-hand knowledge of how to manage a large and complex organization.

The principal figures in Chicago packing on his arrival were Nelson Morris and Philip D. Armour. Armour, to be sure, arrived in Chicago the same year as did G. F. Swift. But he moved from Milwaukee, which had been his headquarters, because the Chicago branch of his business was rapidly becoming of more importance than the parent house at Milwaukee.

Both Armour and Morris had their organizations built and functioning. Behind them were records of successfully operating their large businesses. So their credit was ample.

This was a hard situation for the young Yankee to face in the yards. He never could have overcome the handicap if his entrenched competitors had realized from the start just how serious a problem he was bound to make for them. But even though he was allowed unmolested to continue on his way, he could never have accomplished what he did if it had not been for the long hours he worked and the intensive use to which he put those hours.

His taste was not at all for society. His church alone excepted, his entire interest was in his family and his business. For a good many years the two pretty much overlapped. His whole energy and most of his family's energy went into the business.

Long into the evenings, even after he no longer had routine work to do at home, he lived with it. He was a great man for continuing his day's occupation after dinner, unquestionably one of the things which wore him out.

No doubt there is a great difference between the types of man required to build a great business and to carry it on. He had to work as he did to build Swift & Company. After he had built it to a large and profitable institution, the habit of work was so strongly fastened on him that he could not shake it off.

The rest of us were fortunate. The period of worst struggle, once over, found us young enough to change our working methods to what accorded better with the requirements of the job. I have never since those early days yearned to live all my waking hours with the business. I have been willing to stay at the office as late as anything held me, of course.

But once a man gets away from his office, it strikes

me that he does better to get away from its worries.
His free hours can set his mind off far enough so
that when it comes back to work next morning it
has gained some perspective on the job.

This applies to the established institution. The
owner of an enterprise which is struggling up from
a tiny start to attain its place in the economic scheme
of things can seldom free himself of worries. A
young business requires extra attention just as a child
needs more care than an adult. But when it has come
up to a sturdy youth, then it gets along better with
less than excessive hours of attention. If the owner
has broken off the overwork habit soon enough, he
is of course a whole lot happier.

My father was self-reliant, as are practically all
commercial pioneers. Moreover he wanted everyone around him to be self-reliant. He had little use
for the employee who had to have instructions for
every step in his day's work, or who did not know
how to proceed in an emergency.

He believed in helping those who helped themselves. He used to urge along those of his children
who showed any tendency to turn the other cheek.
"Go after him; don't let him do that to you!" he
would exhort one of the boys and stand by to see
that his advice was taken.

The employee who required a lot of attention and
waiting on did not interest him much. He carried
the same feeling throughout. One morning as he
was driving to the stockyards his horse slipped and

fell on an icy corner.   Half a dozen of horse dealers standing on the corner rushed to the rescue, intending to lift the horse to his feet.

"Let him alone, let him alone," my father protested.   "If he can't get himself up, I don't want him."   Presently the horse got up—a better horse for having taken care of himself.

Absolute honesty like G. F. Swift's is exceptional. Not only did he know that he was honest in all of his dealings, everyone who dealt with him experienced his honesty and felt perfect assurance in it as an unvarying characteristic.   The extent to which some people with whom he did business relied on his honesty and fairness is almost unbelievable.

Consider one incident.   In the days when great quantities of dressed beef were going from North American ports to Europe, we and a steamship company became involved in a dispute involving somewhere above one million dollars.   Settled one way, the transaction would net the steamship line a million dollars less, Swift & Company a million dollars more. The individuals negotiating it were so far apart in their ideas that they simply could not agree on anything pointing toward a settlement.

It had all the ingredients of a fine lawsuit which would drag through the courts for years, yielding tremendous fees to the attorneys.   And word of this went to the steamship line's principals in England.

These shipping men knew my father.   They cabled back: "We will submit this to the personal arbitration of G. F. Swift." It was one of the most startling tributes to character that has ever come to my attention. His decision, granting some things to the steamship company and some to his own company and arriving at an award somewhere on middle ground, was the basis on which the ship owners settled without a question.

G. F. Swift's honesty was not of the sort which took advantage of excuses for not paying over something which belonged to somebody else. To a new employee who had brought him a question of refunding some money to a customer who did not even know it was owed him, father once said: "It isn't mine. I find when it's decided that money isn't mine, I don't have a very hard time finding whose it is." There's a whole practical sermon on honesty in that statement.

Let a Swift employee make a bad trade for the company—he heard from it strongly, from the chief in person. But once the trade was made, it had to be carried through. There was no trying to wriggle out of it. "Lord help you if you tried to get him out of a bad trade by short weight or lower quality!" remarked an old-timer in talking over this characteristic of his chief.

There was in charge of an important department a man who made an especially bad trade for the company on a tremendous contract. Then, some days after he had been told a few things about his chief's opinion of his business ability, he came around with the news that the contract had been canceled by the purchaser, a governmental institution.

We were never able to get to the bottom of just what had happened. It had all the earmarks of someone having cut a sharp corner to get us out of that contract, and there was just one person likely to want to do it. Not long after, this man was let go. But before he was fired, father had warned me about him. "You want to watch that fellow," he declared. "The kind of fellow that'll do that sort of thing for you will do it against you when it suits him to." Anything of a dishonest sort made him distrustful. That the man would cheat for us made him all the worse. Cheating has never been a Swift policy.

Father detested sham and "front." Anything savoring of lying was distinctly on his bad book. He used to spend evenings on end visiting with managers of branch houses and branch packing houses and with executives within the organization. The visit consisted usually of G. F. Swift's asking questions— innumerable questions—and of the visitor's trying to answer them. He would go back and forth over the same ground, coming to it from different directions and checking one set of answers against the others. If anyone attempted to temporize, or to bluff it out, the boss was after him. "Say you don't know, say you don't know," he would impatiently urge the victim of his inquisition. Once he had proved to his own satisfaction that the other man was not a liar, then he eased up on the questioning.

If he found the man was a liar, out of the company he went at the first good opportunity.

He would ask all manner of questions, many of them so technical that no man not an expert on the particular point could answer it. "What percentage of casings are you saving?" he asked one branch plant manager one night.

"I don't know."

"How many hogs does it take to make a bundle of casings?"

"I don't know." (No one not specializing on casings in a plant could possibly know, for it varies with the hogs.)

"Well, I think I'd know that if I were managing a packing house," he would admonish the honest man who said "I don't know." Probably G. F. Swift, with his passion for knowing everything about the business, would have known such statistics as those on casings. But no plant manager could be expected to know them.

"You never felt at ease with G. F. unless you knew him extremely well," is the way one plant manager expresses it. "He was always trying to pick you up. He would ask you questions he knew the answer to, to see if you knew. When he finally made up his mind that you knew a good deal, and wouldn't try to bluff him on the things you didn't know, he took you into his confidence. After that he let you alone with his questions."

His questions always had a definite point, however. He was always digging for something he felt he needed to know. "There's no use fooling ourselves," he would declare to a manager who might protest at the work involved in finding out some fact on which he had been keeping no record. "We might as well find out, then we'll know—and we can't fool ourselves."

"G. F. is the best auditor I ever saw," declared his brother Edwin C. Swift after a long trip with him through a number of branch houses neither of them had ever seen before. "He can get at the facts with questions quicker than anybody I ever knew. And after he gets through asking questions in a branch house, there's no need of going over the books. G. F. knows as much about it after an hour's questioning as an auditor could find out by checking the books for a week."

He was a great man for detail, despite his grasp of the big things in his line. He checked up on literally hundreds of things every time he visited a packing house or office of Swift & Company. One of his pet items was working temperature in the office.

On his way to the manager's office he always managed a look at the thermometer. Coming into the packing-house office in Kansas City one winter morning when the steam was hissing, he saw that the temperature was eighty. "It's a wonder your brains ain't cooked," was his greeting to the manager.

Another time he came into the South Omaha office

with the remark: "Good morning. Too hot in here."

"It's seventy in here, Mr. Swift."

"On what?"

"This"—holding up a thermometer on his desk.

"Is it reliable?"

"Yes, absolutely."

"These others out in the office say seventy-three, seventy-four, seventy-five."

"I know, but this one is right."

"Then what do you have 'em around for?" he protested.

"And you know," the man insists who had the inaccurate thermometers, "that's the first time it had occurred to me that I was not saving money by keeping those things in use!"

A summary of G. F. Swift's personal working methods would not be complete without reference to his thrifty Yankee ways—"his Cape Cod ways," as his managers jocularly called them. Two little incidents, showing opposite sides of his character as it could be seen in a straight business affair and in one tempered by sympathy for those in need, may help to sum up some of the reasons why he was able to build what he built.

His carriage boy usually went with him to hold his horse when he had to go to a meeting. Then at night father drove home, to have the horse available for coming to work next morning. When he dismissed the boy during the working day, he handed over a nickel for carfare to take the lad back to the plant. But when it was after hours he asked, "Going home or to the Yards?"

If the boy said, "Yards," then he got a nickel. If he said, "Home," he got none. Why? Because it would have cost him a nickel to get home from work anyhow. That was the frugal side of G. F. Swift.

Beef for export was shipped in muslin bags. These bags were always made by people who needed the money the work brought in. Chiefly they were made at home on ordinary sewing machines by widows of workmen from the stockyards. Father, because of his intimate knowledge of the circumstances of a great many back-of-the-Yards families, always insisted that he approve the list of those who were to get the work.

One day a man in the purchasing department came to the front office with a proposal that beef bags be made by concerns equipped for doing this sort of thing most economically. We could, it developed, save a good many thousands of dollars a year on beef bags and on the related jobs—which went to the same class of workers—of stringing tags for beef quarters.

"You keep out of this bag and tag business," father directed the employee. "That's something I'm running."

And until export of dressed meat shifted from North American to South American sources, the beef bags were made and the beef quarter tags strung by the widows back of the Yards.

CHAPTER VI

"I VOTE NO!"

MY FATHER doted on frequent reports from weak departments of his business. Not that he found actual pleasure in records which showed he was losing money. But the problems of turning a loser into a money maker involved activity and employing his best abilities. And above all else he preferred action.

He had been brought up on it. He would rather be on his horse buying cattle in the yards than sitting quietly at his desk. But when his business grew beyond the size which permitted him to buy the cattle and boss the skinners, he had to become a manager despite his preference.

His training had been where such things as reports were scarcely known. His beginnings had been small, his development had been through individual enterprises which were almost subvisible when compared to Swift & Company within five years of its start at Chicago. His inclinations naturally held to spreading his time over just as much as possible of the physical equipment of the business, in the idea that only thus could we hope to know what was going on.

But he quickly realized as the business sprang

up to unthought-of heights that he must work out other ways to keep a finger on and in its every activity.

So he became a devotee of reports—weekly reports. "You've got to know how you stand every week," he used to explain. "If you wait a month, maybe you're broke." So he doted on reports, detailed weekly and brought right up to the minute.

His reports came to him weekly as a matter of routine. They were never disposed of as routine, however. A report which can be treated by the executive as routine is a nonessential routine, and probably is better discontinued.

Above all else his favorite statistical diet was the reports of weak departments. His whole being enjoyed the sheer difficulty of going into a seat of trouble, digging out the facts, aligning them, and putting things right. So any losing department had to submit more frequent and more complete figures than did the rest of the business.

The man responsible for the loss had little rest while this persisted. G. F. Swift believed in frequent reminders and in prompt corrective measures. If a loss was not stopped quickly, then something drastic happened.

Once, for example, all the meat in pickle at the Kansas City plant went sour. This meant that we lost the money value of the meat and also the profits on orders we could not fill because of the curtailed supply.

The meat spoiled, of course, because a faulty cure was in use at this plant. Most packers under similar circumstances would have reprimanded the manager and the man in charge of curing so that the trouble would not recur.

Fundamentally, however, the trouble lay deeper than carelessness. The weakness was in the management for allowing to continue a condition which at the time was universal in the industry.

The cures for pork were all secret. The head man at each plant had his secret formula. By paying him a large salary, we obtained his services. These included supervising the curing and personally mixing the pickle. And of course the product of every plant was different. A Swift ham from Omaha was slightly different from a Swift ham from Chicago or St. Joseph or St. Paul or Kansas City.

The unfortunate happening at Kansas City brought sharply to father's mind the fundamental unsoundness of operating this way. So he called a meeting at Chicago of the principal men in the operating end of the business—managers, general superintendents, and so on.

When he had stated the problem, he asked for a vote. The problem was essentially that if we demanded that the formulas be given to the company the men who had the formulas would quit, leaving us in difficulties. Should we demand that they give up their formulas, or should we continue at the old way of doing?

Decidedly the men in that meeting were opposed to taking the bull by the horns. "No," voted each man. Then the chief spoke.

"You've all voted no, because you're afraid to face a little possible trouble. There's no use dodging trouble, if you've got to do things the wrong way to dodge it. You're wrong on this. I'm going to vote yes and it will be yes."

The meeting had, so it seemed to many of the men who gathered there, been called for no purpose. They thought the new rule might better have been promulgated by a general order from Chicago. But in this, too, they were wrong.

Father wanted to hear at first hand just what they thought about the proposed plan. He wanted them to convince him if they were right. Failing this he decreed that the cure used at each plant should be forwarded to Chicago, the best of the formulas selected and made standard for all plants. And by deciding this in the meeting he let those men who believed sincerely in his judgment see for themselves that he was basing his decision on a principle rather than on caprice.

It went through without a ripple. The men in charge of curing at each plant sent in their formulas, despite their many and lusty threats of quitting. The formulas were almost alike in ingredients and proportions. The standard formula was worked out from these. Only slightly modified through the experience of the years this formula is used today as the standard cure in preparing our pork products for market, including our Premium Brand of hams and bacon.

The meeting about secret formulas was not the only one which father ended by voting yes, when the rest of the meeting had voted unanimously no. Because he was dominant in the business, because his ideas generally prevailed—of this, more later—his people from time to time fell into the habit of voting on a business question as they believed he was going to vote.

I recall one meeting where everyone gathered, from his whole attitude, that the chief was in favor of the plan which was up for discussion. So, despite some transparent weaknesses in the idea, they voted yes. After everyone had voted—the votes were always polled singly—the chairman made his announcement:

"I vote no, and the noes have it. You men voted yes because you thought I would. I pay you for your real opinions, not to say what you think I think." It was a good object lesson. It ended the yessing for a good many months.

He was not arbitrary in making these decisions. He had confidence in himself bred of his conduct of the business. He knew the right turn of the road where most of his men must guess on a far less complete knowledge. No wonder he generally arrived at the destination while the rest were wondering what it was all about!

An old plant which had been purchased was to be

extended by adding a large unit. The manager came to Chicago with the plans.

One feature of the blueprints, an open floor for hanging freshly dressed hogs, attracted the unfavorable attention of practically everyone in the meeting. It seemed a needless expense, if not a positive impediment to economical operation. Father listened to the attacks for a while, then leaned back in his chair.

"What've you got to say to that, Johnny?" he inquired of the manager, the son of a Yankee who had come to the Chicago Yards with the original butcher gang from Assonet.

"We can use this open hanging floor for refrigeration three months a year," the manager pointed out—the plant was our farthest north to date. "And it has other technical advantages." He proceeded to enumerate them.

Before he had got well started on the advantages, his chief held up a hand to stop him. "Of course you're right," he decided. The meeting closed right then with the plans approved.

It was not that he wanted his own way regardless. His knowledge was so great that when a practical man was enumerating practical reasons, he absolutely knew. There was no use, therefore, in submitting the plan to further discussion by a number of others even though these others were, after himself, best fitted to judge.

A good deal may be said in favor of this type of meeting after all. It measures up to the ordinary conference as a means of bringing out opinions and information from everyone. And then it leaves the decision to the man best qualified to make it. It puts an automatic stop to buck passing and time wasting, which no business man of experience will deny are the principal products of many meetings. If the top man makes his decision the moment he has the facts at his disposal and then dismisses the meeting, it stops the time wasting before it has a chance to get started. The plan has not been wholly disregarded in our organization since father's time.

Knowledge of every detail of the business was the taproot of his way of managing. His technical knowledge was exhaustive, perhaps as great as that of any man the packing industry has known even to this day. His grasp of the facts of distribution, of transporting the products, of the current standing of company finances—in everything from buying cattle and icing cars all the way through where he would get another ten millions of capital and how he would use it—made him completely the master.

One reason for his mastery of the facts was the time he devoted to business, at the office, at the plants, and at home. Never have I known anyone gifted with such a quick mind who would put in such long hours at his job.

You can rarely talk with anyone who held a place of responsibility under G. F. Swift without there coming out: "I remember one evening G. F. had me over at his house and he asked me—" Hardly an evening that he did not have some of his people at the house talking business and cramming into his already exhaustive knowledge an added store on this point or that—and incidentally giving the employees the benefit of his knowledge and experience.

Talking business was his principal out-of-hours recreation, if it could be called out-of-hours—for he had no hours as working time is generally recognized. The waking day constituted his working hours and he worked at top speed all the while.

One old-timer, a plant man, tells how for weeks on end his chief had him at the house every evening until bedtime. This was in the early days, when the packing house developed new and difficult problems every few hours. Right after supper the plant man would arrive and for perhaps an hour they talked of the day's experience in workrooms and coolers.

Then, the subject temporarily exhausted, father would begin to talk about the export business which was at the time beginning to take shape in a small way but with infinite promise for the future. At least two or three hours he would talk exports to this man who knew slaughtering and dressing and shipping but who had not an ounce of first-hand knowledge on selling overseas.

"I suppose you think it's funny that I get you over here and tell you about all this export business and its troubles," was the explanation which came one night when the practical packer was almost drowsing in his chair from an overdose of exporting. "I'll tell you, I've got it on my mind. I've got to tell it to somebody, and it's got to be somebody I can trust. That's why you get it every night."

For many years we all lived on Emerald Avenue or a block or two away. And "we all" meant the Swifts and the whole management. If a man held a place of responsibility, he lived within easy reach.

The Emerald Avenue location was a neighborhood of better homes than now, of course. But it was never, at best, an especially attractive residence district. When finally G. F. Swift moved to Ellis Avenue, every man of the lot joyfully moved across town to that neighborhood.

A manager or superintendent was supposed to come to the house when he was sent for, no matter what the hour of day or night. And while father aimed to be a considerate man in all ways, he had no respect for idle time. If he wanted a superintendent at 9:30 of an evening for an hour's talk, he sent for him. It would not occur to him that the superintendent would have to be on the plant at 6:30 next morning and that the evening's talk would cut into the night's rest. To any one of his people a night's rest was of no consequence in comparison with supplying information to the chief.

On the evening after the big stockyards strike of 1884 had been broken, principally by father's stubborn stand against the strikers' demands, he called all his foremen to the house. "How many men stayed with you through the strike?" he asked each one. He kept them there until late in the evening discussing their records in holding their men. When he had finished, they had a new comprehension of the value of working with men in the way that wins loyalty.

He was always known as a pusher of men, but never as an inconsiderate driver by the men who remained with him long enough to get really acquainted with his ways. He worked hard himself, harder than he asked anyone else to work. The men who worked with him liked his pushing.

"Don't go to work there, they'll work you to death," a youngster was advised back in Clinton, Massachusetts, when he told some of the villagers he was going to work in G. F. Swift's meat market there in the early '70s. But the boy took the job regardless. He came to Chicago in the slaughterhouse gang which killed and dressed the first Swift beef at the stockyards. He grew up in the harness, became an important man in the company.

"G. F. worked me hard, but he never worked me to death," chuckles the veteran, today retired on his farm from which he frequently comes to visit in the office.

No man ever quit whom father wanted to keep. Probably the chief reason was that if he believed in a man, he would back up that man to the limit. Loyal support from the head of a business makes loyal men beneath the head. And if G. F. Swift did not believe in a man enough to back him up, then he wanted nothing to do with the man.

Certainly in the early days he did not hold his men by paying excessive wages and salaries. He paid small salaries for a good many years. The business was operating on so small a capital and clamoring so insistently for funds that he had to hold down the outgo. He would have been much more liberal if the needs of the business had permitted it. He was more liberal, by far, after the years of greatest expansion were past. But he held his men and kept them working for him loyally and intelligently by the force of his character and the high standards he set them. No one ever attained greater results from his men than he did, principally by the simple expedient of expecting them to deliver more than did other managers.

"No dead lines," was a saying he strongly favored —a dead line was what kept anyone from taking an interest in some activity with which his daily work did not bring him into contact. Everything was considered the concern of everybody. He would not accept the excuse "It wasn't in my department" or "I have nothing to do with the sales department." He wanted no tattling. But he wanted every one of his men to think of himself as a Swift man rather than as a lard department man or a hide cellar foreman or whatever his job.

Because father was the most important individual in the company, every Swift man must recognize a duty to him. That was why a Swift man who found G. F.'s buggy deserted beside a railroad crossing in the Yards was supposed to drive it to the barn.

It was important that the buggy be in the barn ready for the chief's call—and it was the lookout of any employee that it get there.

How deeply this idea was ingrained in father's mind was brought out several times by incidents which in the light of today's attitude toward employees are downright startling. One was a time when his horse, left unhitched before the old Live Stock Exchange Building, took it into his head to run away just as his owner was coming out the door.

Down the crowded street ran the horse, the buggy swaying dangerously through the crowded traffic. Then out from the sidewalk dashed a workman, seized the horse's head, and, after being dragged a few feet, brought the rig to a stop.

Father had been only a few feet behind, on the dead run. He came panting up and addressed the man who had done the risky job:

"What's your name?"

"John Brown, sir."

"Who do you work for?"

With a world of pride in his voice and the realization that he had done a job for which he would doubtless he praised, the man answered: "I work for you, Mr. Swift."

"All right," declared his employer, by now in complete command of the situation. "Be about your business."

Chop-fallen, the workman went back to his job—doubtless believing that he worked for a curmudgeon with not an idea of gratitude in his head. Meanwhile that employer returned to the office, had the man given an increase in pay, called in the superintendent under whom Brown worked, and said, "Here's a man worth keeping an eye on. He just did so-and-so. He thinks quickly and acts quickly. Chances are he'd make a good foreman, first time there's an opening."

As for praising the man for bravery, it never entered his mind. The buggy careening down the street belonged to him, and hence was the particular lookout of any employee. Why shouldn't any man have tried to stop it? The point was that, by stopping it, Brown had shown himself a better man than the mass and hence deserved his advancement. The raise and the recommendation were not, be it noted, any tokens of gratitude for stopping the horse. They were for having the qualities which he showed when he stopped the runaway.

Another man, a clerk in father's own office, was blocked in a street-car tangle on Clark Street one evening. So he got out to walk. As he reached the sidewalk he saw his chief striding along in a great rush perhaps two blocks behind him.

He recognized immediately that his boss had been delayed by the car blockade in getting to his Kansas City train. The clerk knew he had an important appointment in Kansas City early next morning and that he must catch the train. So the youngster ran at top speed for the cab stand of the old Grand Pacific Hotel, several blocks up Clark Street. Then

THE OLD LIVE STOCK EXCHANGE BUILDING, CHICAGO.

jumping in the cab he ordered the driver to make fast time south.

Sure enough, he soon saw the tall figure of his chief striding along, at every step looking eagerly for a cab—and with very little chance of catching one in that latitude. The clerk pulled the cab up to the curb with a flourish. "Jump in, Mr. Swift," he directed. "Get to the Union Station in three minutes," he ordered the driver.

"Mr. Swift never said anything to me about that," says this man, who today occupies a place of large importance with us. "I knew it was regarded as a good piece of work, and I suspect it was behind a promotion which came to me soon after. But as far as G. F.'s attitude toward me was shown, he expected that sort of service from his people. Of course he knew he didn't get it from all of them, so when he got it he marked the man responsible as worth watching in future. But as for thanking the employees— that would have placed the whole transaction on a false basis."

He was, in his relations with the people under him, as in all his relationships, absolutely and meticulously fair. But he was never guilty of letting anyone believe that he expected from an employee anything less than the utmost. That would not have been good management.

Just as he did not believe in praising a man, so he did not believe in bestowing large titles on employees. He was so much and so thoroughly concerned with the realities of earning profits that the surface froth did not enter into his calculations. One of the surest ways to arouse his irritability was by going to him with such a question as, "What shall we call Mr. So-and-So's new assistant?"

"I've got no use for them titles," he would exclaim in some wrath, waving the interrupter out of the office with gestures of impatience.

Very few indeed were the titles bestowed.

Father harbored another deep conviction. "Swift & Company can get along without any man, myself included," he remarked a few times in my hearing. "This business will be bigger after I'm gone—that's what I'm building for."

It *is* bigger since he is gone.

But I know that it could not have become so big and so successful without the impetus it received from his management. Nor could its growth have been so steady and healthy, lacking the heritage of sound management methods and management policies which he built and gathered for it.

CHAPTER VII

HE HAD TO SPREAD OUT

WHETHER right or wrong, father *would* expand his business at every opportunity. He was a born expansionist.

But he was not a plunger. He knew his business, knew it intimately and in great detail. Because he could see where others could only grope, his vision was steadily ahead of his time.

"That crazy man Swift," the wiseacres called him when he came to the Yards from the East and set his whole energy and twenty years' saving to accomplishing something at which everyone else had failed. No one had succeeded in shipping dressed meat east and disposing of it at a profit. It was one of those things which everyone knew couldn't be done.

His partner Hathaway, of the Boston firm of Hathaway & Swift, could see no chance for success —and Hathaway had been in the live-stock business a good many years longer than had his younger partner.

Hathaway knew, as did everyone else, a thousand reasons why nobody could sell Chicago-dressed beef in the East, and why the East would continue to eat meat from cattle shipped alive for slaughter at the point of consumption. So vehemently did each feel himself right that the partnership had to be dissolved, though with no break in the friendship.

So the younger Yankee was left to build himself a business, to build it on his dream and his accumulated capital of thirty thousand dollars—which was not enough even in 1875 to operate the smallest conceivable packing plant for thirty days. He started under the handicap of inadequate capital. He was not willing as so many men are willing to give his capital a chance to catch up with the size of his business. He could have done this in the first very few years after he succeeded in accomplishing "the impossible." But he *would* keep spreading out.

Always his vision ran ahead of his fellows, of his competition, and of his capital. Always he had under way some enterprise which strained almost to the breaking point the supply of working funds he could command. And despite this ability of his somehow to keep ahead of financial difficulties, his mind ran ahead of his financing ability—he felt himself held back because he had not enough money to do this or that. It was always so.

Even if he had lacked his insistent urge to expand, he would unquestionably have become a successful packer. His other abilities were too great for him to have made anything short of a success. It was his creed of "Expand, and then some more," which kept him from using his $30,000 to build one of the smaller packing establishments, one of the scores doing a profitable business in tens of millions of dollars.

This creed it was which built him one of the very few transacting a volume in the hundred millions.

He always had an eye for business beyond the ken of others similarly situated. He was only nine years old, as a relative tells the story, when he walked into his grandfather's house and said, "Grandpa, I'll give you forty cents for the old white hen."

"All right," agreed his grandfather—and with no more ado the boy paid his money and went to catch his hen.

"Isn't that new business for Stave, buying hens?" inquired an older cousin who had been completely ignored by the nine-year-old intent on his job.

"Why," the grandfather answered, "he is here almost every day after one. He finds a customer somewhere. Seems to get enough out of it to pay."

There had to be some way for the boy to make money, if he was to have any for himself. Certainly there was no surplus for distribution among the twelve children on his father's sandy, unfertile Cape Cod farm. The best paying crop on Cape Cod today—almost the only paying crop—is summer boarders. For a good many years after Gustavus F. Swift's birth in 1839 the summer boarders had not begun their annual migration.

The boy saw little that was promising in life as a butcher's helper in a Cape Cod village. He had gone to work for his older brother Noble at fourteen and by his sixteenth birthday was making—be sure that he was earning—three dollars a week.

Even in those days of 1855 the golden goal of ambitious Cape Cod lads was Boston. He began to lay his plans for a move to Boston and the West.

His father objected. He saw for his son no great future in the big city, equipped as he was with no fund of education, of business experience, or of demonstrated ability. He held that strong sixteen-year old country lads were a drug on the Boston market. To back up his ideas he was willing to do a fair share —more than a fair share, perhaps, when one considers the value of a cash dollar in his circumstances of life.

"You really want to be in the meat business, don't you?" he questioned his son. "All right, Stave, I'll give you twenty-five dollars to start up in the meat business around home. That way you can get your start right here, instead of going away to the city."

With this twenty-five dollars was started the business which is today Swift & Company. The lineage is straight as an arrow. For, twenty-five dollars in his pocket, the boy of sixteen set forth to enter the meat business.

He made a neighbor an offer for a good fat heifer he thought he might butcher to advantage. It is characteristic of his shrewdness as a trader—shrewdness as far above his age as was his shrewdness above other business men's thirty years later—that he did not, boylike, offer his whole twenty-five dollars. Whatever his original offer, he actually purchased the heifer for nineteen dollars, as he told the story in

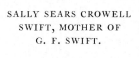

SALLY SEARS CROWELL
SWIFT, MOTHER OF
G. F. SWIFT.

WILLIAM SWIFT, FATHER
OF G. F. SWIFT.

later life.   He drove her home and slaughtered her in a shed.   Now he was embarked in the retail meat business.

He cut up the beef, loaded the cuts into a wagon of his father's and set out to sell the meat in the neighborhood.   Fortune favored the enterprise, another way of saying that he had used good judgment in buying the heifer, ample skill in cutting up the carcass, and sales ability in disposing of the cuts.   He netted ten dollars out of the transaction for his time and trouble.   Forthwith he went out to repeat the operation and the resultant profit.

For a few weeks or months he had ample capital— the only time in his business career when he had, except for the last two or three years of his life.   But soon that active mind of his began to see larger opportunities which called for more working funds than he had been able to acquire by selling pot-roasts and steaks and ribs.   He could always see the chance to make more money by doing on a larger scale.

The first occasion of this sort has been told by a cousin of my father's, E. W. Ellis, sixty-five years later.   Thomas W. Goodspeed set it down[1] as follows:

"He called on Uncle Paul Crowell (son of Grandfather Crowell and village storekeeper).   I obtained this information a few days after from Uncle Paul himself.   Stave said, 'I want to borrow some money. Will you lend it to me?'

[1] *The University of Chicago Biographical Sketches,* Vol. I, p. 176.

" 'Oh,' said Uncle Paul, 'how much do you want?'

" 'Four hundred dollars,' said Stave.

" 'Whew,' said Uncle Paul, 'what you going to do with it?'

" 'I want to go to Brighton stockyards and buy some pigs.'

" 'Why, that will be quite an undertaking for a boy.'

" 'Yet,' said Uncle Paul to me, 'I could but admire his ambition.'

"Brighton yards, located northwest of Boston, sixty miles distant! Just imagine it! The worst kind of sandy, crooked roads. . . . . Well, in about ten days, he, with his drove, hove in sight at my father's home. He had sold some, but about thirty-five shoats were still with him. I looked over his outfit, which consisted of an old horse and a democrat wagon in which a few tired or lame pigs were enjoying a ride and a rest with their legs tied together. With him was another lad as helper, who was trying keep the shoats from straying. There was Stave, a tall, lank youth, with a rope and steelyards on his shoulder, also a short pole he carried in his hand that might do duty to suspend the squealers and steelyards between his shoulders and those of his customer. Father said: 'There is a good exhibition of ambition. Gustavus Swift will make a success in whatever business he undertakes. For he has the right make-up.' Gustavus made several such trips to Brighton for pigs, spring and fall, for two or three years."

The occupation of drover under these conditions was at best highly seasonal. Outside the spring and fall months, he might have lacked occupation. Instead, he worked out a procedure which gave him a business. He arranged for quarters at Brighton stockyards where he could slaughter his animals.

Each Friday he bought a steer on the market there and slaughtered it on Saturday. The quarters he hung over Sunday. Monday morning bright and early saw him in his democrat wagon with the meat, bound for Cape Cod. By Friday he had sold his beef and was back at Brighton once more, making his weekly purchase of one animal.

From his repeated Monday-to-Friday trips the young man accumulated a little money—a very little, no doubt, but enough to give him a foothold as a retail meat dealer instead of a wagon peddler. So he opened a market at Eastham, which shortly afterward he turned over to his brother Nathaniel. Then he opened a meat market at Barnstable and settled down as the meat dealer for this town of five hundred.

Father and mother, Annie Maria Higgins, had been married during the short career at Eastham. At Barnstable they and their growing family—there were four of us children by then—remained some eight years. But it was not the retail business which held G. F. Swift. Rather it was a broad business he had developed, leaving the market to be run by a clerk. Once more he was at his habit of expanding.

Beginning as he had at sixteen and continuing

without interruption as a cattle buyer, by the time he moved to Barnstable he had become an extremely good judge of cattle. There is no way to check up on the accuracy of a cattle buyer's judgment except to see how his purchases dress into beef. Even though his career had been active for only six or seven years, father had been seeing how each one of his cattle dressed—not only seeing it but also feeling with his own pocketbook the results of his judgment. In a man of his shrewdness the only possible result was that he became a remarkably good cattle buyer.

With his knack of seeing the opportunity for broadening out his activities, he had no sooner been set down in Barnstable than he began to wonder if he could not market Cape-Cod-raised cattle at a profit. The average farmer had only one or two head for sale in a season. The nearest market, besides the small local butchers like himself, was at Brighton beyond Boston. And it didn't pay to drive just one or two head to Brighton, even as low as the farmer valued his time.

So once more G. F. Swift ramified his business. To be sure, he kept the meat market, but this was now a side issue. He became a cattle dealer, buying on Cape Cod and selling at Brighton.

It is noticeable that, however he might expand or diversify his interests, he never deviated by a hair's thickness from the original direction of his work. Ever broader, ever making a little better living, ever building up his capital but spreading it just as thin as he safely could, he was on his way to founding the modern dressed meat industry!

By 1869, when he was thirty years old, he had accumulated enough to take his first step of any size. His capital was far from a fortune; it had taken him fourteen years to expand his original capital of twenty-five dollars into a sum sufficient for anything at all extensive. With this capital which he had sweated out by working sixteen hours a day father opened the meat market at Clinton, Massachusetts.

This enterprise has been described earlier in this book. It was a large store, for that time and place a pretentious, ambitious store. It developed quickly into a large and profitable retail business doing an annual volume of thirty-five or forty thousand dollars. It yielded him an income which in those days was unusually good for a small town.

But hardly had he attained for his store the momentum he had planned when his mind grasped other opportunities. Being a retail meat dealer involved pretty much killing his own meat animals and selling the cuts a few pounds at a time. But there were growing up, in some of the more thickly populated districts such as that around Boston, wholesale slaughterers and wholesale meat dealers who supplied neighboring retailers fresh dressed meats, thus saving the storekeeper the job of slaughtering.

Father was not unaware of this development, and of the related development which involved a shift of source of meat animals from local raisers to the grazing districts of the West. The ratio of cattle population to human population of the New England states had declined far below the point of domestic supply. The cattle to make up this deficiency were coming in from the West, which meant that someone was making a profit in handling them.

Never did a significant trend of any sort within the live-stock or meat industries escape G. F. Swift's alert mind. He saw a chance to become the slaughterer and wholesale supplier to his neighboring retail meat markets. Soon he was doing a considerable business in selling to the trade.

But even this development, with its improvement of a business already to be counted good, did not hold him for long. He had attracted the attention of two of the prominent figures in the New England live-stock and meat businesses. One was D. M. Anthony, a large wholesale slaughterer and meat dealer of Fall River. The other was J. A. Hathaway, a cattle dealer most of whose animals found their way aboard cattle ships bound for England from Boston.

Anthony wanted young Gustavus Swift in with him. So did Hathaway. The upshot was that the Clinton business was turned over to Edwin C. Swift to manage. And two new firms came into existence: Anthony, Swift & Company, of Fall River; Hathaway & Swift, of Brighton.

Shortly thereafter we went to Brighton to live. Father sold his retail market at Clinton to a man named Pope, while my uncle continued to manage the Clinton wholesale business. All of the Clinton butchers who were not needed for the wholesale business were now transferred to Anthony, Swift & Company's slaughterhouse at Assonet, just outside Fall River.

"Well enough" was never satisfactory to Gustavus Swift. He had been at Brighton only a year or two, buying cattle for Hathaway to ship and for Anthony to slaughter, when he decided that the advantageous way to buy cattle was near the source of supply. A big stockyards had been established at Albany. So he moved us to Albany, a peg nearer the source of supply.

However good Albany had looked to him as the primary market when he was doing business in eastern Massachusetts, it looked nowhere nearly so fine after he was on the ground. To be sure, cattle were there to be dealt in in great quantity. But to his analytical mind it was not right as a primary market.

He followed the railroad back to Buffalo, where another large stockyards was running. He kept taking short trips there to look over the market and to buy a few cattle. Buffalo was better than Albany, because it was nearer where the cattle came from. It left a good deal to be desired, though. Chicago was yet to be inspected.

The more father thought about Chicago, the more logical it sounded. The cattle on their way from the farms and the ranches and the plains made Chicago their first stop. Then why was not Chicago the place where, inevitably, cattle could be purchased to the best advantage? At Chicago must be the greatest selection, with the minimum of commissions and handling charges accrued against the animals.

So in 1875 he came to Chicago. Here he bought cattle for Hathaway to resell, for the Anthonys and Edwin C. Swift to slaughter and sell at wholesale. He also purchased cattle in Chicago on commission for Calvin Leavitt & Son, of Brighton, which sold these cattle to the Brighton butchers.

Wellington Leavitt, who is now and for a great many years has been Swift & Company's head cattle buyer, was the "Son" in the firm of Calvin Leavitt & Son. When Wellington Leavitt was still in business at Brighton with his father, he helped sell cattle sent down by my father from Chicago.

What cattle G. F. Swift purchased at Chicago that summer of 1876 all went east in cattle cars. But he conceived the idea of slaughtering the cattle at Chicago and shipping only the edible parts. Why pay freight on a thousand-pound steer? That steer would dress down to six hundred pounds of beef. Most of the remaining four hundred pounds were thrown away or were even an expense because some-one had to be paid to cart them off.

Father tried it experimentally the next winter. He shipped box cars of dressed beef. Some of the cars were heated by stoves to prevent too hard freezing and accompanied by a man to tend the fires. Other cars were shipped with no stoves, completely

WELLINGTON LEAVITT, (LEFT) DEAN OF THE CATTLE BUYERS, WHO BECAME ASSOCIATED WITH G. F. SWIFT ABOUT 1875, THE PRINCE OF WALES, AND LOUIS F. SWIFT RIDING THROUGH "THE YARDS", OCTOBER 13, 1924.

dependent on the weather. All of the cars came through in good condition, with the beef all the better for hanging several days in transit.

From this the step to refrigerator cars was, in time, short. In difficulties it was long and wearying, too long for discussion at this point.

Every step of it, however, involved expanding, involved spending more money, involved a larger volume to make possible the savings or the profits or whatever the objective was for which at the moment he was striving. He had to lay all of the groundwork himself. No one else could obtain the funds he needed. No one else could improvise the thousand and one successful expedients which kept his business going upward.

For he kept the business climbing. Rather he raised it to ever higher points by projecting his creative imagination upward from one stage to the next, then taking the leap and carrying the business with him.

And he held absolutely to his own business. This is a basic reason why he succeeded in building up his business so fast. He went, everyone knows, at a rate considerably faster than a conservative man would have thought either possible or safe. He held absolutely to his own line. He knew what he was doing and why. His decisions were based on a meticulous knowledge of his own affairs and of the whole industry. He built in his own way and didn't wait until the time when he would have the money.

Each step of expansion was a definite progress along a charted road. Father had no idea at the outset that his business would or could become as large as eventually it did. But he was heading it always in its given direction.

He developed the idea of shipping beef instead of cattle. Right there he unquestionably selected his goal. He determined to head those who purveyed meat to the public.

He set his heart on being the leader, he set his mind to becoming the leader. This would have seemed a preposterous dream to anyone but himself, considering his lack of money and backing. No wonder they called him "that crazy man Swift." But if to others it seemed overreaching, to father it seemed so wholly reasonable that he attained leadership by a route straight as an arrow. He went that route, he reached his goal by strength of will and determination.

All circumstances were with him—particularly the times. If he had not exploited the refrigerator car, someone else no doubt would have succeeded with it in at least a few years. Others had already had some success with refrigerator cars without attaining leadership in the industry. With his early control of large-scale use of the refrigerator car and his remarkable combination of ability and energy, father had an advantage which he crowded to the limit. This limit was the leadership of his field.

How he pushed for sales outlets has already been described. His personal working methods by which during the early days he concentrated sixteen or eighteen or occasionally twenty-four hours a day on overwhelming problems which harassed him—these have been told in a previous chapter. The summer of 1875 had seen the thirty-five-year-old Yankee come to Chicago's Yards as a late entrant in a race which seemed already settled. Fifteen years later he had sales branches or dealers in every strategic city of the United States. He was shipping great quantities of meat abroad in refrigerator ships. He had outlets all through the British Isles and in many Continental cities.

No longer was his enterprise confined to beef. He had put the company into mutton, into pork and provisions, into all of the by-product lines which had been an essential outgrowth. Swift refrigerator cars rolled by the thousands over every railroad in the country.

It was toward the close of the '80s that he raised the question of building branch plants still nearer the source of supply than Chicago. Beef cattle were coming principally from the West and Southwest. Why not slaughter them near their points of origin and thus effect savings comparable to the savings which had been attained when beef was dressed at Chicago instead of at Fall River?

At Kansas City, Kansas, was a stockyards of considerable size. Several concerns were operating packing plants there, one or two of them on a reasonably large scale. It was selected as the site of our first western branch. In 1888 the Kansas City plant went up.

It provided an excellent market for southwestern cattle. But Kansas City was not the most economical point for stock from the plains of western Nebraska and Colorado and the country farther north. So the Kansas City plant had been operated for only a few months when an identical plant was built at Omaha. The Omaha plant was completed in 1890. The plant at East St. Louis, Illinois, was finished in 1892.

The panic year 1893 gave the building program a set-back. But after a few months to recover his wind, father was once more aggressively at his plans for expansion. His next step was the St. Joseph, Missouri, plant, finished in 1896. Its start and its subsequent history well illustrate his way of tackling a problem when it presented itself to him.

St. Joseph is between Kansas City and Omaha. It is far less important as a railroad center than either of these larger cities.

An earlier effort had established the packing industry at St. Joseph, but while it had managed to struggle along it had not thrived. Kansas City with its large live-stock market offered stockmen a better chance to sell their animals. At Kansas City, buyers were actively competing and huge numbers of animals were dealt in daily.

At St. Joseph, only sixty-five miles away, there was little activity. Grass was literally growing in the yards there. The local business men earnestly

G. F. SWIFT, ABOUT 1885.

wished to bring in one of the larger packers with a large plant. And they approached the head of Swift & Company.

He did not want his information or opinions at second hand. He went to St. Joseph, taking with him a few of his lieutenants, and was feted and argued at. But all of that rolled off his mind like so much water.

It was at a banquet given him in St. Joseph that he made one remark from which has echoed many a chuckle. Frogs' legs were part of one course, but the guest of honor refused them.

"You'd better have some, Mr. Swift," urged one of the local hosts. "They're very tender."

"They ought to be," the partisan of beef came back at him with some heat. "All a frog does is sit on the bank and sing!"

Not the entertainments, but the personal investigations of himself and of his men, finally induced his decision. He studied the town, the people, the character of the country. For several days he drove around the surrounding country by himself or accompanied by that one of his own men who could contribute the most expert knowledge of whatever point he was studying.

The character of the soil. The local crops. The number of bushels to the acre. The kind of roads. The kind of farmers. The way the railroad layout would permit shipping stock to St. Joseph. All these points he studied until he probably knew a good deal more about them than did any local banker or other man around St. Joseph.

His investigations showed him that, even though it was within sixty-five miles of Kansas City, a good market at St. Joseph would divide the Kansas City and Omaha hog supply. He could buy the St. Joseph stockyards, which would give him an advantage here.

Everybody considered it a wild enterprise, even most of the men most closely associated with him. But the chief had made up his mind. "Folks think we're a little bit crazy," he told the meeting which had gathered to consider the purchase. "But there's lots of live stock down that way. They haven't got a real market there, so they don't get the animals.

"If we set out to make a market there, we'll make a market. We'll buy the stockyards and put up a plant."

It looked like a foolish move. The St. Joseph plant was built over the objections of a large share of his organization. But it paid—paid well. Like many of his most profitable expansions, in advance it seemed to almost everyone else absolutely wrong. He was simply ahead of the rest of us. He grasped all the facts and correlated them into a plan which brought dollars into his stockholders' pockets.

Immediately after the St. Joseph plant came the plant at South St. Paul. Here was a defunct packing plant which he bought because he saw something that others could not see.

People thought hogs could be raised only where

corn was grown—and the country around St. Paul was not then notable for corn. But father never did much loose thinking. He had a scientist's passion for indisputable facts. He checked up and learned that the farmers there had screenings and other small grains which did not grade up well. Consequently a farmer could more profitably turn this into pork than he could sell it as grain.

He was right. Almost invariably he was right in anything bearing on his affairs. Now South St. Paul kills more hogs than any other Swift plant except Chicago, which has of course remained the largest plant in every respect.

G. F. Swift could see further into the packing industry's future than any man I have ever known. He was very much the expansionist all of the time. He saw cheap live stock and he could not keep his hands off it. He had to expand to get facilities he felt he had to have—and he expanded so intelligently that he reached exactly the point he was aiming for.

Nothing was too big for him if it looked to show a profit. Sioux City stockyards offer an illustration. There had been a top-heavy boom at Sioux City, financed by eastern money. In every direction the plans had been laid along most ambitious lines—and eventually it blew up, of course.

Father wanted the stockyards. The creditors would not sell the stockyards separately. They would sell everything to one buyer or they would sell nothing. So he bought the whole thing, paying a large sum of money and taking along with his stockyards a number of enterprises he had no use for.

Here once more nobody would vote with him. Everyone knew he was wrong. But his vision showed him that the stockyards alone were a good buy at the price he had to pay for the whole—even if he had to throw away everything else about the property. As it was, the facilities which were not needed were gradually sold off, the last parcel years after his death. But as he had foreseen, this was an excellent buy. Today the stockyards are worth considerably more than he paid for the whole property. What he and subsequently his estate sold the rest for was clear profit on an already profitable deal.

Always he kept his affairs ahead of his finances and his plans ahead of his affairs. One reason, the principal reason he managed to carry the thing off, was that he knew his business and held to it exclusively. He had no interests outside live stock, packing, and closely related enterprises. A secondary reason why he succeeded where most men must have failed was that he knew the measure of everyone from whom he borrowed money in any considerable amount. The lender acted as the borrower counted on him to do every time.

When father started at Chicago in 1875, those in a position to size him up swore he would fail. When he began to expand, the dire prophecies were quite as confident. But he made every enterprise successful with which he was connected.

At the outset, he had about thirty thousand dollars from his share of the partnership of Hathaway & Swift. In 1885 his firm was incorporated as Swift & Company, with three hundred thousand dollars capitalization. Within two years he had to recapitalize for three millions, so rapid had been the young company's expansion.

By 1896 the capital stock was fifteen millions. By 1903, the year of his death, the capital was twenty-five millions. And every cent of the capital had come either from earnings or from subscriptions at par by existing stockholders whenever a new issue was made. The company's total sales in 1903 exceeded one hundred and sixty million dollars. Its president had seven thousand employees under him by that time.

For Gustavus Franklin Swift, while a dreamer and a visionary, based his dreams and his visions of expansion very much on the practical facts of life.

CHAPTER VIII

"I RAISE BETTER MEN"

"THERE'S an ice house down at Beardstown
might be a good buy for us," G. F. Swift instructed one of his young men some thirty-five years
ago. I want you to go down there and look it over
carefully. Get the facts on its dimensions, ice capacity, construction, and everything else important."

So the youngster journeyed to Beardstown, spent
the better part of a day there, and next day presented
himself at his chief's desk. He reported a great assortment of facts.

Finally the boss interrupted him to inquire, "What
kind of drainage is there off the roof?"

"Drainage?"

"Yes, drainage. What kind of spouts, gutters,
and so on?"

The ice-house expert got red in the face. He did
not answer.

"All right, now, you don't know, you don't know,
do you? You get right on the next train and have
another look at that ice house. When you come back,
you be able to tell me all about that roof drainage
and anything else you think maybe I ought to know
that you don't know now."

So back to Beardstown the young man traveled.

He spent a day going over the ice house a second time. Half the day he spent on the roof. Next day he was back to report once more.

"You went up on the roof this time, didn't you?" inquired his chief after listening to a detailed description of every foot of tinsmithing about the premises.

"Yes, sir."

"I wanted to get you up on that roof," he declared with a dry chuckle. "I wanted to get you up somewhere near the top of this business. There's only one way a fellow like you can get to the top. If you don't do your job any better than you did first time I sent you, the only way you'll get to the top is by running the elevator."

Another time father was coming from the East to Chicago on a train arriving at night. At Cleveland the manager of one of our wholesale markets got on the car, going to some town near by. His chief joyously cornered him at once and began asking questions, as was his habit with any manager he ever succeeded in getting off by himself.

All went smoothly for a while. Then the boss asked, "How many windows on the west side of your cooler?"

"I don't know, Mr. Swift."

"Don't know! I never heard of a branch-house manager who didn't know how many windows he had in his cooler! You get off this train, go back to Cleveland and find out all about those windows. I'll expect you in my office at Chicago tomorrow morning to tell me how many windows there are and anything else I ask you. I guess we're slowing up now. See you in the morning." And he blandly waved the bewildered manager off at Sandusky.

Next day the man appeared at Chicago and underwent a rigid examination on all of the details of his cooler and its peculiarities. What's more, word of the episode spread through every Swift channel in the country. Managers who valued their peace of mind knew, thereafter, how many windows their coolers had. Moreover, they knew a whole lot more about their physical equipment than ever before.

At handling men, at selecting them, at training them to places of real responsibility—at all of these duties father's ability was superlative. His methods were in large measure unconventional. By their very lack of resemblance to the time-honored and time-worn they were the more effective.

When he sent a man back to have a second look at the roof drainage of an out-of-town ice house the employee learned for all time that on any assigned job he must do just as well as any man could. What is more, this lesson made him into a first-rate head of the ice department—a position into which the man developed and which he filled creditably for many years.

At one stroke G. F. Swift taught this lesson to a good many people besides the particular man who had to make the second trip. Because the punishment was so picturesque and at the same time was both laughable and appropriate, the story was passed along from employee to employee. It was something to chuckle about—and while he chuckled, every Swift man worth his salt applied to himself the standard of performance toward which the parable pointed.

The branch-house manager who returned home to count the cooler windows went for a parallel reason: a manager ought to know all about the equipment he is in charge of. The method the chief used here was almost exactly the same as that applying to the ice-house roof. Yet I dare say no thought of it came into his mind when he ordered the manager off at Sandusky. His mind worked so directly on a specific problem in handling men that he arrived forthwith at the proper answer. That the problem was similar accounts for the similar solution.

Father frequently asserted, "I can raise better men than I can hire." The proof of the assertion is in the present-day proportion of men trained under him who are in positions of high responsibility with Swift & Company more than twenty years after his death. He trained his men—"raised 'em," as he used to say—by methods which are as sound in principle now as they were then. Obviously some of the details would not fit this generation, which stubbornly believes that the boss is not invariably right.

A man who later had charge of one of our most important activities recently told of an experience with his chief forty-odd years ago. He had come to work just before Christmas of 1884, at a weekly wage of fifteen dollars. He had made a strong effort to get seventeen when he was hired, and failed. So after a year he asked for the two-dollar raise.

"G. F. took me out in the hall," he tells the story, "and walked me around a corner to a window. I can see him yet, as he put his cowhide boot up on the window sill and looked down his nose at me. 'You think you're worth more money'n you're gettin', do you?' he inquired rather savagely.

" 'Yes, sir,' I assured him.

" 'Well, you're not,' he told me. And then he started in to tell what he thought of me as an employee. It took him a long while. I had felt pretty sure of myself before I tackled him for the raise and I had a lot of good reasons why I deserved it. But I never got a chance to use them. He told me what was wrong with my attitude toward my work and he illustrated the general statements with specific examples out of my short career with him. He used the examples liberally, yet managed to give me the impression he had a lot more in mind which he wasn't citing because of the short time at his disposal for so insignificant a task.

"He literally took my hide off and nailed it to the door. When he got through with me, I felt real gratitude that he still tolerated my unwholesome presence in the office and was willing to let me continue drawing the same old fifteen dollars a week.

When he had finished the job, after an hour and a half or perhaps two hours, I went back to my desk and went to work. I was full of the idea that I was next to useless. But G. F. had left a ray of hope in parting. He let me believe I might have a chance to become a productive member of the community if I really buckled down to the job of putting into use some of the advice I had just received!

"A year afterward, I got my two-dollar raise without asking for it. After that I steadily went along, taking on more responsibility and drawing bigger pay. It was some time after G. F. had raised me to ten thousand that he inquired very casually one day, 'Remember that time I took you out in the hall over in the old Exchange Building and told you what I thought of you?'

"I had supposed he had forgotten it years before. 'Yes,' I admitted—and I could feel myself getting red around the ears with the memory of it.

" 'Do you know why I did it?' he asked me.

" 'The only reason I know is that you were mad at me because I had been doing such a poor job,' I told him honestly.

" 'Why, no. That wasn't it at all,' he explained in some astonishment that I had not comprehended it long before. 'You were doing right well for a young fellow. Not bad at all. But I thought you had the makings of something better than an ordinary clerk and I wanted to see. I jumped on you that day just to put your feet on the ground. It made a man of you, that talk did. I could see it by next morning.' You know, I think he was right!'"

Father did not believe in sparing overmuch the feelings of the man who needed correction or guidance or reproof. He felt that if a man needed talking to, the talk had better be strong and to the point. In these days employees were less sensitive, their sensibilities had not been so assiduously cultivated. Consequently his specific ways of going at such a job roughshod did the minimum harm and the maximum good.

But even though his methods would require some alteration to be usable today, the principle on which they were based is just as sound as ever it was. The man who hears promptly and forcefully about a mistake of procedure or of judgment has been caught at the right time and in the right way to make him remember the lesson. If he is the right kind of man he is better off for being corrected.

It is remarkable to look back now and see how large a proportion—how unbelievably large a proportion—of the men who came in for father's reformative measures have come up and up in the ranks. Some of the men he started in on could not stand the treatment and dropped out. Most of those who stuck it out became real assets to the company and have been rewarded accordingly.

Yet it was not always easy to reconcile a spirited man to treatment which he might feel was nagging. Those of us who were very close to G. F. Swift and had worked with him over a long term, knew that he never nagged. It was a mark of distinction to any man to have his chief return time after time to point out that individual's shortcomings and general uselessness.

One youngster was working as an assistant of mine when some failing or other brought him to father's attention. The boy was in a position where he was responsible for the work of a sizeable group of people, many of them a good deal older than himself and longer in the service. Consequently when he undertook to change their ways he had his troubles.

What caught the chief's eye was something that the youngster's subordinates were doing wrong. I happened to be out of town, else the first reproof would have come my way. As it was, he went after my helper.

It was his fashion, once some wrong method or weak spot claimed his attention, to check it up daily. The youngster did not make very fast progress in correcting his people's fault. So every evening, along about closing time, he was sent for. When he came to the front office he received a talk on his weaknesses as a manager. Finally the chief saw that some resentment was smoldering. So he inquired, "You think I've been after you pretty hard, don't you?"

"Yes I do, Mr. Swift."

"Well, I'll tell you. If you work for me long enough, some day you'll know something and you'll be some good to somebody." That was G. F. Swift's

idea of a handsome way to make amends for all he
had said before!

Finally, after ten days or so I returned from my
trip. The youngster was just waiting for me to return
so he could quit. But I had one argument that
changed his mind. "Father doesn't go after a man
day in and day out if he thinks he's wasting it," I
told him. "You sit here every day, you hear the way
he goes after me, so you know you aren't getting half
as much scolding as I am. He's pretty careful about
not going to a lot of trouble to correct a man if he
doesn't think the man is worth correcting."

Before long the youngster was sent to England on
a particularly important job—at the chief's suggestion. A little later he had to do some more foreign
traveling. While he was still in his early twenties he
was untangling hard knots for us all over the world.
Today he is operating one of our largest plants. He is
a fair sample of the results father got by his methods.
They were effective even though they sometimes
seemed harsh.

I doubt whether G. F. Swift consciously thought
of himself as a teacher in his job of training executives. Certainly he was about the most effective
teacher I have encountered. And while he was a
terror to the man who was weak or wrong, he was
extremely helpful to the man who tried hard.

One plant manager says of him: "When I first
started to work in a place where Mr. Swift saw me,
I was afraid of him and would go out of my way to

avoid him. But after I really knew what I was doing, I especially wanted to see him when I came to Chicago. Before I planned a trip definitely I would generally try to find out if G. F. was planning to be there. Even when I didn't have any one thing to take up with him, I wanted to see him. For I knew that in the course of our talk he would give me some idea or other which would be valuable— more valuable than anything I was likely to get elsewhere."

When any of the leading men of the branch houses or even one of the more important beef salesmen came to Chicago, that man stayed at his chief's house. The custom had its start in the early days when transportation from the stockyards was slow and difficult, so that for convenience the men had to be kept at the house instead of being sent to downtown hotels. It was continued because father liked to keep right on with his business after the evening meal and he saw a really valuable way to employ this time in talking with his out-of-town men.

He would question the visitor by the hour until he had satisfied himself that the man was honest and knew his job. Then the more intensive questioning ceased. But in the earlier months of a man's tenure of his new job, every visit to Chicago meant so many evenings of cross-examination.

One new manager after his first experience of this sort went back home and prepared a good-sized pocket notebook in which he kept facts and figures of all sorts that his chief might require. A traveling auditor or someone of the sort brought back to Chicago word of this loose-leaf ready-reference compendium. It appealed to everyone, including father, as a huge joke. Thereafter he was extra careful to ask this man unusual questions. Tradition has it that for three years the notebook was maintained, that every time its owner came to Chicago he kept his hand on its reassuring bulk in his coat pocket—and that not once in that time was he asked a question for which he had the answer in his book!

After a new man in a new job had established himself as worth educating, his employer would proceed with the training. One of his methods was to go over a batch of random mail with the visitor, especially in the later years of his life when he used to have some of his letters sent over to the house. He would ask the guest what he would do about this request for charity, about that application for reinstatement. After a session like this the employee had a grasp on some of the basic rules of business which he had never before comprehended.

Once G. F. was convinced that a man should develop into someone of consequence, he kept trying and trying to do the job. It was seldom he failed. But occasionally he had, after a long struggle, to give it up.

There was one such man he sent to St. Joseph as assistant manager. The newcomer did not fit in and after a while was transferred to Kansas City. No matter how much time his sponsor would spend with this man, he could not bring him up to the mark. Also he kept trying to get both the St. Joseph manager and the Kansas City manager to say that the fellow was some good. Finally he gave it up. But he hated to do it.

"There isn't much use giving up a man too early if you think maybe he's going to be all right," he observed on this occasion and a good many times after. It became one of his precepts in developing men.

If he once sized a man up as having possibilities, he would not easily change his opinion. Occasionally this wasted a good deal of everyone's time in trying to develop a man who would not develop. Also it lost just so many months in getting the right man on that job. But more time is saved by patience in training men than by impatience. Few traits cost employers as much as the common failing of giving up a man for hopeless long before he has proved it. We try to inculcate in all our people this idea that there is no use giving up a man before he has proved himself worthless. As a result we develop the latent ability in a good many men and women who would not last two months if we were critical in the early stages.

In general father was not much on hiring men from the outside for jobs of any consequence. He preferred hiring his men young and bringing them up by hand. His inclination was to hire competent

men on the outside only when they were especially
equipped for some new enterprise with which we
lacked experience.

Occasionally, though, he stepped right across the
line and hired someone for a special reason. When
our plant at St. Joseph was building, he made the
acquaintance there of an eastern man, O. W. Waller,
who was having an uphill fight to make his little
packing plant break even. Father developed the
habit of dropping in on Waller for a visit after his
list of duties in St. Joseph had been completed and
he was ready to leave by the first train.

One evening their visit continued until about half
an hour before time for the Chicago train. It happened that Waller was also going to Chicago but had
said nothing about it. Instead, once the caller was
out of his office he hustled out the back way, jumped
into his buggy, and drove home for dear life. At
home he changed his suit, packed a bag, ate a hasty
supper, and was driven up to the station platform at
a gallop just as the train pulled in.

Quite a party of us were going in on that train,
but father was fascinated by the performance of his
rapid-moving acquaintance. It was so wholly like
his own way of arriving with never a minute to spare.
He deserted his own forces for the companionship
of the St. Joseph packer after introducing us singly
and recounting the speed with which this gentleman
had traveled once he got started.

They sat together during all of the evening, in the

course of which father reminesced in great detail
about his career from the age of nine down to date.
This of itself was so unusual that we were all astonished. As they said good-night, father told him,
"Any time you want to come to work for me, I've
a good job for you."

Not long afterward Waller gave up the fight. He
had not been able to overcome the handicaps of inadequate capital and inefficient plant. No sooner was
he announced as going out of business than the head
of Swift & Company was after him to take a job
with us. Waller's ability to accomplish a great deal
in a short time was so remarkably like his own that
father recognized he would fit well into a place of
responsibility.

So he was sent for to come to Chicago. And all
around the offices the chief introduced him to everyone as "Mr. Waller from St. Joseph, who's come to
work for Swift & Company."

"But I'm not working for Swift & Company," protested Waller.

"You mean to say you wouldn't work for us in the
right kind of a job?"

"What kind of a job?"

"Manager of a packing house."

"It might be all right, if it was the right packing
house," admitted Waller. "What one did you have
in mind?"

"St. Louis."

"I wouldn't go there on a bet."

"Will you go for six or eight weeks?"

"Why, yes, if it's only for that long."

"I thought you'd go to St. Louis," exulted his new boss. "After that the new plant will be ready at St. Joe and you can take it."

So Waller went to St. Joseph as manager of our newest branch plant. He went on the chief's say-so and pretty much over the judgments of the other men well up in our councils, for he was a new man with us and it has never been our policy to put outsiders over old employees if the job could possibly be filled from within. But this once, G. F. Swift was convinced that he had hired a better man than any of the "raised" variety who were available. And he stuck to his conviction.

Because he did not want to take a single chance of being wrong after he had put an outsider in this place without consulting the judgment of his lieutenants, the boss proceeded to devote special attention to Waller. For the first year or so the St. Joseph manager was frequently summoned to Chicago and father went often to St. Joseph.

Since then Waller has occasionally told of his long sessions with his chief. From dinner time on, every evening in Chicago was devoted to talking over Waller's management problems, the affairs of the one plant and of the company. Father was always ready to counsel with him—though, in all justice it must be said there was no need for paying any extra attention to him. As usual, the head of the business had been absolutely right in his size-up of his man. Yet Waller declares today, no doubt correctly, that his lightning-like activity in catching the train at St. Joseph is alone what attracted the attention of G. F. Swift and brought about his offer of a good job.

In the early days the business kept calling for more and more men as it grew, and its head had to hire a good many men outside. His trade was shooting upward so fast that even his ability at training executives could not keep up with the demand. So he was always picking up likely looking men and putting them in training for jobs that needed filling.

For example, there was a grocer near where we lived. He had a good enough little business as neighborhood grocery stores went. But that discerning eye saw in him the material for a bigger place than ever his little store would afford. Father therefore advised him to sell his business and come to work for us.

First thing we knew the store had changed hands and the man was working in our wholesale market. He learned there how a wholesale market is run and the points which need watching. Presently he was going around our branch houses checking up on the managers, helping them to build up to the standard maintained in our Chicago packing-house market and picking up from all of them hints which he might pass on to the rest so that the wholesale organization would run more smoothly.

G. F. Swift's standing and reputation were such

that many a man gave up his own established business to come to us, with full confidence that he was bettering himself. That is how L. A. Carton came as treasurer in 1893 when the financial end of the organization loomed too big for its founder's continuing attention. It is how a good many of the best men came in the early days.

The man who could do better than most men some task which was part of our function was a man to catch his employer's attention. In the first years of the business this is how a good many of the men were found on the outside to take places of responsibility with us. All the way through it has been how men inside the organization have been chosen for larger positions.

There was one young man who came as a clerk in the president's office. At first his duties were chiefly filing. But he showed a real knack for keeping up with the work and for finding letters or contracts on the instant. Moreover he displayed an intelligent comprehension of the fact that he was there to save his chief's time and energy. Several times he used unusual gumption under circumstances where he might have been excused for letting things slide along.

So his boss noticed him. And one day when his secretary was away, with the youngster taking hold of the work as best he could, a cable announced that a ship which we were counting on to carry a load of beef to England had gone into dry-dock at

UNION STOCKYARDS, CHICAGO, 1927.

Liverpool and therefore could not meet its scheduled sailing date from Boston.

The schedule of sailings was handled in that office by another man under the secretary. The secretary always checked over this man's work and then submitted it to his chief. So the youngster turned over to the expert the job of rearranging the schedule of sailings.

But when it came to submitting this to the chief the expert would not. He was downright afraid, with that bone-quaking fear some clerks have of the big boss. So the report had to be taken in by the younger clerk, with the expert hovering in the background to handle any overtechnical questions.

Right away, of course, there came a question fairly bristling with technicalities. The spokesman said, "I don't know about that, Mr. Swift. Brown here can tell you."

"So you don't know, eh?" inquired the boss pleasantly. "Well, I don't know as I'd expect you to know all about that. But if you're going to come in here with reports you've got to know all about them. I don't want to have Brown explain it, as long as you're the one that's bringing it to me. You go along now and find out all about it. Probably Brown can make you understand it. After you do, come back and tell me. I expect to be in all morning. And if we come to something else you don't know, why I guess we can give you some more time to find that out."

One secret of his success in training men was the way he dealt with them. He knew all about practically every detail in the business, the standards to which every operation must be held. His microscopic eye for detail never overlooked any really significant points, even though he might not concern himself too immediately with them.

When he wrote instructions to a manager or a superintendent, he was explicit. Usually he closed such letters with the injunction: "Please answer and say if you will carry out these instructions." That phrase, winding up a letter, leaves no doubt in the recipient's mind as to what is expected of him.

At the same time, given a man in whom he had confidence, he would seldom overrule that individual's deliberate judgment. He preferred to let the man incur a loss, if necessary, to prove to his own satisfaction what would always have remained a doubt if it had had to be accepted on his chief's say-so. And he was seldom so cock-sure that he knew he must be right and his employee wrong.

The manager of a middle-western plant found a good market in San Francisco for dressed poultry. After a few experimental shipments he sent a man there to look after the dressed poultry business on the coast and one day mentioned to his chief that this had developed into a nice profitable venture.

It was the first father had heard of it. "You'll not make any money shipping poultry to San Francisco," he assured the manager.

"But we're making money at it now," was the rejoinder.

"You'll not make money on it in the long run."

"Do you want me to stop shipping and bring that man back here?"

"You'll not make any money at it."

"I think we can make money at it, Mr. Swift. Do you want me to stop it?"

"Oh, let's talk about something else," suggested the boss.

For a long while we made money at it. The manager was right, even though father had been so sure about it. His unwillingness to order a manager to go against his own judgment was one reason why he built up throughout the world a corps of representatives who handled his affairs superlatively well.

CHAPTER IX

THE FORBIDDEN YARDSTICK

ALL his life G. F. Swift was developing at a prodigious pace, developing in mind and skill and knowledge. Quite as naturally as a boy attaining manhood loses his awe toward many unremarkable adults who a few years before towered above him, so father found his standards always changing.

Men whose technical skill at one time represented his highest ideals of attainment became a few years later to his fast-marching mind a pack of fogeys. His own development had meanwhile gone to a point far beyond the ken of the mossbacked gentry.

First and last a good many of his men, most of them a deal younger than their employer, left him because they had failed to keep within hailing distance as he progressed. It took a nimble wit and a lust for hard work to hold that pace. Not that he expected every man to keep up with him. But the man in a key position—be he a department head or a superintendent or a clerk in the president's office— that man kept step or stepped out.

Only a good man could suit him for long. Father was sizing his people up all the time. He watched their performances in comparison with one another and in the light of what he knew about their abilities.

"The best a man ever did shouldn't be his yard-stick for the rest of his life," was the maxim and the working rule by which he managed his men. The department head or superintendent who used that forbidden yardstick was not worth keeping.

Even more than in developing executives—and he excelled at it—G. F. Swift's knack of dealing with human beings appeared in his work with the rank and file of his employees. After all, it is easier to build up alert, ambitious individuals into competent executives and managers than it is to get a reasonable degree of work and intelligence out of the ninety-seven per cent of employees who never develop the capacity for authority and who never can. For the individual of managerial caliber is the exception and will do his best to help you push him ahead. The majority of inert people on the pay roll have an uncanny gift for using just enough gumption to hold their jobs and win little promotions, but they never show the traits which bring a man major responsi-bilities and major rewards.

The man of initiative and common sense quickly gains enough experience to appreciate the reasons behind his own promotions and reprimands. But the fellow down in the lower ranks of the business is usually more of an individualist. He lacks the training; and he has never tasted the rewards which come to one who subordinates personal preferences to the group's welfare.

Whether it was in the earlier days when father was

dealing direct with his workmen and clerks or whether it was in the later years when he could plan only the general policies, he displayed a genius for handling employees. To people in Swift & Company who did not know him well, or who had not worked with us long enough to understand what was at the bottom of his relationship with employees, the head of the business sometimes seemed an unpleasant, hot-tempered boss. He was unquestionably sarcastic. Sarcasm was his tool for keeping his subordinates alert and free from mistakes which should not be repeated.

But his irritability (as it seemed to some employees) arose out of disappointment. He was really disappointed, with a sense of personal error, when he found a weakness in an employee who he had not expected would have that particular failing.

One plan he followed constantly to minimize expensive errors was to get reports on all claims allowed our customers. These reports came to him on large sheets with brief particulars of each claim. Each summary described the error behind the claim and told who had made it.

Whenever he found a few unoccupied minutes in the day, he sent his office boy for a claim-sheet offender. Into his office would march some clerk he had never seen before. The culprit always knew, from the time the claim was allowed, that eventually he would be personally called to account by his chief.

Father would sit there for a moment sizing up

the man responsible for the loss. To the clerk it unquestionably looked as if his employer was racking his brain for a refinement of ingenious punishment. Actually the boss was looking him over to see whether he looked like a man who would habitually make mistakes and whether he was worth trying to save. His tendency was to err on the side of charity, to give the man a chance to make good.

After a moment he would speak. "So you're the young fellow who ordered out five hundred pounds of leaf lard and two hundred and fifty pounds of compound when a customer had bought two fifty of lard and five hundred of compound?"

"Yes, Mr. Swift."

"I suppose you know the customer claimed he used it up just the same way as if he'd got what he ordered and we had to bill it to him the way he ordered instead of the way we shipped?"

"Yes, sir."

"I suppose you think it doesn't make any difference if you make mistakes like that. Doesn't make any difference to a big rich company like Swift's if it has to allow a customer a claim of $13.47. We'd be in a fine fix if everybody made that kind of a mistake once a month, wouldn't we?"

The employee who emerged from the encounter with the least damage and still on the pay roll was the one who did not try to excuse the error, who acknowledged it and showed by his demeanor that he recognized it as a serious offense which he would carefully guard against in future. The man who tried to be flippant, or who took the attitude that anyone was likely to make mistakes and that a certain number of mistakes was allowable to any man—that fellow was likely to be through in a hurry.

Father did not consider any mistakes allowable in a well-managed business. That was his base on which he built the whole structure. He knew that errors would continue to be made. But none were allowable and no one would be retained who showed too strong a tendency to lose us money.

This is one of the really sound principles of business management. No mistakes are allowable and every mistake must be regarded as a serious lapse. If any other attitude is taken toward errors, then there is no controlling them.

It is always necessary to draw a definite line somewhere. It is impossible to draw a definite line on errors unless it is drawn right at the source. Allow it leeway in the slightest and it will move steadily away in the direction of more mistakes. And it is mistakes which lose money for a business.

If a concern is engaged in a sound line of business and if some fundamental change such as a new and monopolized invention which could not be prophesied does not render it suddenly unsound, then it may in general be said that it will always make money except when someone makes a mistake. The mistake may be one of judgment, of wastefulness, of carelessness, or whatnot. It may at the time seem important or unimportant. But the most basic mistake of all is to condone mistakes.

Twenty or thirty years ago it was no doubt easier to hold employees to a strict accountability. Discipline in the office and in the packing house was almost as strict as discipline in the family. And back in the '80s and the '90s the head of the family was obeyed or there was real trouble! Discipline was a part of the working code rather than a tradition of bygone days.

Father was a strict disciplinarian. Not always did his disciplinary measures bring about the results he had counted on. But he kept working along the same lines nevertheless.

He was walking through the cellars at one of our western plants one day with the superintendent when a negro trucker passed, whistling loudly. "Stop him whistling, stop him," the chief directed. So the superintendent called, "Hey, Sam, no whistling on the job"—which was the first ever heard of this on the plant in question. And the chief added, as explanation to the surprised negro, "If everyone whistles, we'll have no order."

A few minutes later they went to the hog-killing floor. The hog house was small for the plant and everything was done by hand.

The gang was composed of stalwarts every one—most of them southern negroes, with a few Irish at pivotal points. The day's schedule was six thousand hogs, a big day's work. Someone had started the negroes singing when the whistle blew that morning and the work had been turned out six hundred hogs an hour, ten a minute, right from the start.

"Here! Here! Stop it!" the astounded visitor had to shout to make himself heard over the ringing chorus of "Down in Mobile." So the superintendent called the foreman, who immediately silenced the singers.

"That will slow up the work, Mr. Swift," the superintendent told him. "We want to get out six thousand hogs today and we'll never do it without the singing. It helps those boys work."

"Never mind," directed his employer. "I think we can kill the hogs without any musical accompaniment. Yes sir, we turn out a lot of pork at Chicago without singing."

"You have conveyor chains, rolling tables, all the other facilities at Chicago for speeding up the work. If you need to turn out a little more than the usual production, you speed up the conveyors a little and the men speed up to keep pace."

"I think we don't need the singing. It's bad for discipline," was the final word on the subject.

But along later in the day as the visitor and the plant manager entered the superintendent's office, that practical soul took from his desk the production reports which had been accumulating during the day. They showed that from the moment the singing had stopped hogs had been killed at the rate of four hundred an hour instead of six hundred as before.

He handed the sheet to his chief without comment.

"Hm," came the decision after a considerable pause. "Hm. I guess maybe there's a little something in what you say. Maybe you might let those boys sing when they've got an extra lot of work to do. But—" regretfully—"it's mighty hard on discipline."

One of the cardinal principles which enabled him to raise better men than he could hire was his sparing use of compliments. He believed in seldom praising. His creed held that if a man does good work he deserves no praise for it, it is exactly what he is paid to do. If his work is exceptionally fine, still don't praise him. Give him a raise and a better job with more responsibility at the first chance. Thus you give the man the benefit he has earned by his ability. You have, as an employer, advantaged yourself of the employee's capacity. And you haven't spoiled him by telling him he is good.

The good man who came to us from another concern was likely to have been told that he was good and consequently to have had his head just a trifle inflated. The man who knows he is good is likely to be a bit sensitive about how he is treated. He requires an amount of dignity to support his best work. Father had his attention centered only on getting the work done and he had no time to think of useless frills. He did not build up non-essentials by compliments. That is one way he raised better men than he could hire.

He tried his best to hold his managers to the same point of view. He did not want them upsetting the apple-cart by giving out praise. Once at St. Joseph he was going over the plant with the manager when they encountered a negro janitor engaged in some job which, while it had to be done, yet was outside a janitor's regular duties. The manager praised him for his alertness in seeing the need and pitching into the job on his own hook. As they walked away he said to his chief, "There's one of the best men on this plant. He's always surprising me by doing better than I can expect anyone to do."

They walked on for a minute or two in silence. Then from the depths of his experience the older man offered his comment: "You're going to spoil a good boy—spoil a good boy, Mr. Donovan."

At another plant he was going through with a younger man, a foreman who has since become a plant superintendent. As they were standing by a long zinc table where they were doing the scraping by hand, he inquired, "Mr. Pratt, where do you think these hogs should be cleaned?"

"Right here where they are being cleaned," answered the foreman.

"We don't do it that way at Chicago," retorted his boss—this was the reply he used to squelch anyone at any of our other plants who stood up for an inferior way of doing. Chicago was at that time supposed to include all packing-house virtues developed to date. The other plants were the provinces.

"There are a lot of things you don't do at Chicago," replied Pratt. "We're scraping them while they're still hot from the scalding water. At Chicago they scrape the hogs on the rail. I think this is a great deal better than the Chicago way."

"Young man, you're right," his employer admitted. This was the highest praise he could bring himself to administer.

The veteran who went through this experience laughed about it many years later. And he commented: "I believe this is the only time Mr. Swift ever agreed with me about anything we discussed! Next time I was in Chicago, a few months later, I observed that he had them handling their hogs by our method."

It is noteworthy that the chief did not tell the man his idea had been adopted. He knew the originator would see it some time at Chicago. Meanwhile there was no use acting as if the man had done something to make a fuss over.

But if G. F. Swift was sparing of praise, he was lavish with advice about better ways to do things. He never overlooked an opportunity to instruct.

"How do you think these hogs are dressed?" he inquired of a plant man on another trip.

"I think the day's killing is well dressed," the employee told him.

"I beg to differ with you. That's all,"—and he waved the younger man back to his work.

Next day the plant man received a letter from the

plant superintendent, with the president's criticism attached. Busy as he was, father had gone into great detail about how the hogs should be opened straight through the center of the aitch-bone, split to show the loin and fin bones equally on each side of the hog, and the button of the neck split in the center. It was a constructive set of instructions on one operation of pork packing. Giving instructions took up a much larger part of his usual day than did praise.

One thing he insisted on was absolute honesty. Time and again he came to my desk or called me to his and pointed out some slip-up in shipping dates or a let-down in quality or something else which had the appearance of a sharp corner having been cut to get an advantage for Swift & Company. He would lecture me on the specific mistake. But always he would end up by talking about the need for being absolutely fair and honest all of the time. "We want character to go with our goods. And sixteen ounces is a Swift pound." I don't know how many times he said this to me; it must have run well up into the hundreds.

So it is not surprising that in the early days especially, before the spirit of fair dealing had been absorbed by all of our people, a good many men got through in a hurry. Usually it was for a lie or for misrepresenting to a customer. Father had no use for anyone who had any other standard than absolute honesty and sixteen ounces to the pound.

I recall one man who was fired for stealing. He

appealed to the front office. "I've worked for you for twenty years, Mr. Swift," he pleaded.

"You stole, didn't you?"

"Yes, sir."

"You worked for me twenty years too long then," was the decision.

There was another man, manager of a branch market, who got to drinking and committing a lot of the faults which so often accompany this overindulgence. He was sent for.

"Mr. So-and-So, how do you like working for Swift & Company?"

"Oh, very well, Mr. Swift." The employee went on to enlarge on the virtues of the house.

"You like your job, do you?"

"Oh, yes, I'm very well satisfied. I'm trying to do my very best. . . . . " and so forth. The chief waited for him to finish.

"Well, you've been doing a lot of things you hadn't ought to, a lot of things we don't stand for. I'm glad you liked your job, for you ain't got it now." And the man was through.

This kind of discipline was not inspired by any desire to be unkind. There was none of the cat-and-mouse idea in inviting the man to come from his eastern branch to be fired and in asking so solicitously after his liking for his job. Father knew the story would run through the whole organization and serve as a reminder that employees were not encouraged to behave themselves in ways which interfered with their usefulness. It was stern discipline, but effective.

Yet, rigid as were his ideas of discipline, he allowed them to relax for the worker who had earned special consideration or about whom there was some reason for not holding to too high a standard of expectation. There was a coachman who was discovered getting away with a little money.

Mother simply sent over to the cashier at the office when she needed money. This had long been the custom. The cashier handed over the money and charged it to "G. F. Swift Personal." Almost anyone was sent over from the house on occasion and the cash was always handed over—sometimes in rather larger amounts than the servant who got it was used to handling.

When the coachman was discovered knocking down money under this plan, he decamped. Father had him brought back by the police. And then he began thinking about how unbusinesslike the whole arrangement had been, how unfairly it placed temptation in the servants' ways. He couldn't keep the man in his employ. But he dismissed the charges against him and worked out a voucher system which made it unlikely that any such thing would happen again.

Another time the head of the ice department went to his chief to tell his suspicions that an old-time employee assigned to a minor but trusted place in his department had been dishonest. The old-timer was being used to pay off the ice-harvest gangs, always in cash. There was at the time no way to check up whether his payments and his amounts drawn for the purpose tallied.

"I think he's taking all of the ice-gang pay-roll money that's left after he pays off," the manager explained. "He isn't turning any in. Of course he may be carrying over the surplus from one gang and using it to pay the next, but I doubt it."

"The chances are he ain't," father admitted. "You know, he never had a very good education. Don't know the difference between his money and mine. But he's been a good faithful servant here and we can't expect maybe that he ought to be trusted with cash. He's always got a job here, though, as long as he lives. We may have to guard him from temptation, but he's always got a job here."

I think it is generally agreed by the men who worked with him that Gustavus F. Swift was one of the fairest, squarest bosses anyone ever had. He treated everyone alike, whether the employee was a member of his family or someone who had been placed on the pay roll only a week before. Some of us, in fact, suspected that he was more lenient to the ordinary run of employees than he was to his near relatives.

He was very much interested in the personal affairs of his people—a goodly amount more so than some employees thought was any of his business. He realized that a man's personal habits had a great deal to do with his ability and also that they shed light on what might be expected of the individual. When an employee got a share of Swift stock, the president of the company was likely to check up a year afterwards to see if he still had it. If it had been transferred, then he wanted to know why.

He wished his people to own stock. He was a pioneer in bringing this about in a big way. His was the first large concern to encourage its employees to become substantial stockholders.

A typical instance of the way he did it was when he called in one young man who had been with us for about a year. The youngster was doing well and gave every indication of becoming a valuable man. "Are you intending to stay with us?" was shot at the boy.

"Yes, Mr. Swift."

"Well, you seem a likely sort of young man. Maybe I'm mistaken, but it looks to me as if you might develop into someone who'd be of some use around here if you stay. Now, I want to have my young men partners, even if they can't do it in a big way. Like the idea?"

"Yes, sir."

"We're going to increase our capital stock. Got any money?"

"Only about two hundred dollars."

"All right. You can buy a thousand dollars worth of this stock if you want to. Pay down what you can and give me your note for the rest. I'll carry it for you and you can pay me off as fast as you're able."

So the employee got the stock. He still has it, I think, along with a good many more shares. That he was a likely young man was proved when he developed into a department head, then went abroad in charge of a substantial share of our business.

Father never overlooked an opportunity to place a few shares of stock with his people. When there was no other stock available, he would sell a little of his own to the employee, replacing it at the first good opportunity. But all of the time he kept in mind that the employee who is a partner is usually the keenest to make money for the firm.

Likewise he recognized that the concern which is owned by a very large number of shareholders is more stable than the company which is closely held. And its stock is more difficult of stock market manipulation.

Next in desirability as stockholders he rated customers. Swift stock was originally bought by eastern live-stock and meat men who constituted our first body of customers, the nucleus around which our dressed-beef business was developed. When new outlets were added, either as dealers or as agents, the newcomers were given the opportunity to buy a few shares. Thus the sales organization was built up with an undivided loyalty and a desire, founded on self-interest, that the company prosper.

I have said that sarcasm was my father's working

tool in handling employees. He might be and he generally was very personal in his remarks, but he meant them impersonally. No matter how hard he jumped us—I got just as large a share of this as anyone else—he left us with the feeling that it was all deserved. He left no sting but he left us convinced. No matter how hard he might jump, no matter how wholly unpleasant he might be in the tenor and tone of his remarks, next time he saw the employee the storm had blown over. The man who weathered one such talking-to generally got through any of its successors without having his feelings seriously abraded.

Another of his knacks in raising better men than he could hire was his ability at cross-examination. Whether the questioning took place in his office or at home or at the employee's desk or workbench, the procedure had its common characteristics. If the chief was seated, he looked as if he had been poured into his chair. He slumped down with his weight on the small of his back. But no matter how indolent his appearance, his lively blue eye kept roving.

His first questions would be so unrelated that the employee would wonder what on earth the boss was driving at. His succeeding questions would begin to shape up into a skeleton so that the man began to think he knew what it was all about. And then, when the conclusion seemed right ahead and the employee felt himself safely exonerated of all blame, father would with one or two well-placed queries turn an abrupt corner and skewer his victim neatly

THE FARM HOUSE AT BARNSTABLE.

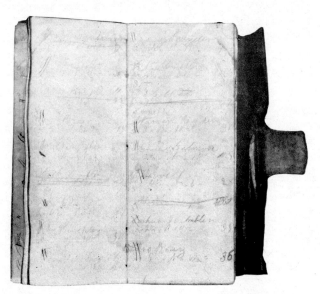

G. F. SWIFT'S ACCOUNTS, 1859-60, RECORDING
SALES OF MEAT FROM HIS BUTCHER CART.

on the sharp point of the cumulative admissions which conclusively convicted the man of something he had not even known he was suspected of. Never did G. F. Swift's questions indicate the direction in which he was working, until he had the answers so well in hand that there was no use denying his conclusions. His method might conscientiously be recommended to any earnest prosecuting attorney!

But if his questionings were devious, his instructions to employees were always direct. He said absolutely what he wanted done, in as clear-cut a way as anyone could devise. Then he left it to the employee to work out how he would get the results.

He was the driver, the dynamo of the business. He worked his men hard and treated them fairly. From time to time I have heard rumors of this or that employee who felt himself badly treated by father. But whenever I have been familiar with the facts, they have been all on the employer's side.

One instance was a man who came to us at a good-sized salary to improve our office routines. He was recommended as a first-class man and so represented himself. But like most men who set themselves up as experts, he soon showed that he knew considerably less than the good practical office men we had with us all of the time. So father had him fired.

Presently he appeared at the front office and was admitted. He was tremendously angry. He had, so he claimed, been hired for a year—and here he was fired within two months. "You're not getting the results you said you'd get, are you?" his employer inquired mildly.

"Not yet. But I was hired for a year, Mr. Swift."

"All right," the boss assented—not showing by his actions or manner what he thought of someone who failed to deliver what he had agreed to, but demanded his pay just the same. "You go over to Mr. So-and-So in the packing house. He'll have a job for you."

A telephone message got there ahead of the office man. When the one-year employee arrived, he was given a squeegee and instructions to keep the blood running into the blood-gutters. After a few hours there he had enough, even though he would have been drawing his stipulated pay as an office expert.

I have no doubt that this man felt terribly mistreated. There are instances of this sort which give rise to lurid tales of G. F. Swift's terrible temper and rank injustice. But I have never found a basis for it.

Over against this we can set the statement of a man who worked with him from the start at Chicago—who came out, in fact, from the slaughterhouse of Anthony, Swift & Company at Assonet to take charge of slaughtering at Chicago. He left us in 1897 to take a position with another concern which could temporarily afford to pay several times as much as we could for his specialized ability. Thereafter he had no connection with us, no reason for telling a good story about us.

It was almost thirty years after he left us and

fifteen years after he retired to live on his income that he told a man unconnected with our business:

"I worked for G. F. Swift for twenty-seven years. He was the squarest man I ever worked for. All that time I never asked him what he was going to pay me. I never had cause to complain. If you worked well for him, he saw that you got what you deserved in money and in every other way."

There, it seems to me, is the basic explanation of father's oft repeated assertion:

"I can raise better men than I can hire."

CHAPTER X

FIGHT WHEN YOU MUST

IF INDUSTRIES have birthdays, all record of them is usually lost in the snuffed-out memories of the dead. Seldom can you put your pencil on the yellowed page of an ancient calendar and say, "On this day began such-and-so an industry." These birthdays are difficult to mark.

But the birth record of the packing industry may be here written down with certainty and in no fear of contradiction. The modern dressed-meat business was born on the day after the Assonet butcher gang came to Chicago.

It was an autumn day of 1876. These Yankee butchers who had worked for Anthony, Swift & Company just outside Fall River came on a Grand Trunk pass, as was general in those times. Next day they fell to their task in the shed—by courtesy called a slaughterhouse—which G. F. Swift had purchased from one Billy Moore in preparation for their arrival. The lard refinery of the business he founded stands today on the site of Billy Moore's unprentious establishment.

The day can be marked as an industrial birthday because the beef those New Englanders slaughtered was placed in a box-car and shipped back to their home town.   From this start came Swift & Company.   I think we are not boastful in feeling that with it began the modern packing industry.

It marked a definite era in father's business career. It meant that he foreswore the live-stock business which during most of his life had been his livelihood.   Instead of live stock as the merchandise he dealt in, he was substituting dressed beef.   Because he envisioned an industry shipping beef from Chicago to feed the eastern states, he made dressed meat an industry.

His partner, D. M. Anthony, of Fall River, agreed with him—agreed, however, with a reservation of enthusiasm.   Anthony was willing to risk a little money on his partner's idea, but he was not giving up his profitable going business to undertake a crusade for a new idea, even though that crusade might, as he hoped, turn out a moneymaker.

J. A. Hathaway, father's partner in his other firm of Hathaway & Swift, had no faith in the idea.   It is not remarkable that he had not, for he was a cattle dealer.   Anthony, a slaughterer and meat dealer, might have been expected to show more interest in a means of making money for handlers of meat. Hathaway could only look on it as an unsound plan. If this unsound plan should by any chance work out successfully, he knew it must ruin his line of business.   It is human nature to take little stock in anything which might cost you your living.

Hathaway and his partner differed so radically on

this question that they dissolved their partnership. Their viewpoints could not be reconciled. Hathaway came to Chicago, paid cash for his partner's share of the joint interests, and returned to his cattle business at Brighton. He brought with him from the East a financial statement on which to base the settlement. "How do those meet your figures?" he inquired of his partner.

"I don't agree with you," the younger man told him. "I don't agree with you at all."

"Why, I'm surprised," declared Hathaway. "I thought I had my figures right. How far are we apart?"

"One cent. Your figures give me one cent more than I'm entitled to."

So they parted the best of friends. The older man brought along two gold watches. One of these he gave to father and the other to mother. They were fine watches and were treasured always as a memento of a friendly partnership which could not be continued.

Gustavus F. Swift was not a man who had many quarrels. "Use tact when you can—fight when you have to," was one of his working maxims. He always preferred going around a difficulty to going through it. He never threw a challenge into the other fellow's territory until he had made up his mind that arbitration or compromise would not settle the trouble.

One result of his tactful ways was that he had only

two serious labor troubles during his lifetime. The first of these was in the '80s, the other was the Pullman strike of the early '90s. With neither of these was he specifically concerned as an opponent of the strikers' demands. But when the strikes came and he saw that tact would no longer serve, he swung into the job of fighting with every resource he had.

If the disputes leading to these affairs had arisen out of conditions directly under his control, there would have been no strikes. When, however, the strikes threatened his prosperity through no fault of his own, then he proceeded to do everything he could to break them.

The first was a bitter strike. Particularly in those early days, father could not afford a shutdown and the consequent loss. He moved into the stockyards men who would work in spite of the strike. And he got his foremen to exert every influence to keep their men at work.

He was pretty well recognized as a leader in breaking that strike. Broken it was. After it was over, the foremen who held any considerable proportion of their men were noted for meritorious service. Not a few individuals who later rose to important responsibilities owed their promotions to the attention they attracted by holding their men at work.

The Pullman strike was altogether different. It was aimed not at us but at the Pullman Company. Its net result was to prevent the free movement of freight—which in the packing business means a

shutdown in short order. The strikers were determined that cars should not move. G. F. Swift had a
stubborn streak when anyone tried to tell him what
he could not do. His determination matched the
strikers'. He refused to be buffeted about in the
rôle of innocent bystander.

The crisis as it affected us came one day when getting the cars rolling was especially important to us—
it was July 3, or the day before Memorial Day, or
some such occasion. The trainmen of the railroad
which switched cars in the yards had been intimi-
dated. Trunk railroads, however, were under United
States military protection. If the cars were once
placed on trunk line tracks we were reasonably sure
they would reach their destinations.

So we organized an impromptu train crew, with
guards, to move the cars from our loading docks and
turn them over to the Michigan Central. Richard
Fitzgerald, president of the Chicago Junction Rail-
way, lent us a switch engine. An old employee who
knew the workings of a locomotive served as engineer. The rest of the crew was made up of one or
two high officials, such as the general superintendent,
and the whole Swift family, including father.

To the accompaniment of jeers and, be it confessed,
an occasional brickbat, we switched a train of refrigerator cars out of the stockyards onto the tracks of
the Michigan Central. There a yard engine was
waiting to take them. Then we all went back on
the engine and tender and repeated the operation.

Feeling ran against us among those who sympathized with the Pullman strikers. A few of our empty refrigerator cars were burned up and a few cars of beef likewise.

But the meat kept moving out of the Yards—and when President Cleveland called out the United States troops from Fort Sheridan to protect lives and property, the strike was soon broken. It was a daring move for a man in political office. I can think of few who would have done it, however much right was on the side of law and order as against the strikers.

Difficulties with transportation had been father's daily portion almost from the time he came to Chicago. As soon as he began shipping dressed beef he ran into snags which were skillfully placed in his way. The railroads, in short, did not want his dressed-beef business. They wanted to continue hauling live stock, which gave them about double the tonnage. The basic idea of slaughtering at Chicago and shipping beef east was to avoid having to pay freight on the inedible portions of the cattle and to avoid the loss of weight to the cattle, due to the hardships of travel. But the railroads had not yet been educated to an appreciation that what is economically sound is in the long run most profitable to the carriers. It was this lack of understanding which eventually brought upon them the first governmental regulation.

Rate making in those days of the '70s and early

'80s was almost entirely a matter of bargaining between the individual shipper and the carrier. The Interstate Commerce Act had not yet appeared. And the carriers would not bargain on dressed-meat rates. They simply set a high rate and sat tight.

This was the group of old railroads, comprising the Trunk Line Association, which have the direct routes from Chicago to the East. They got the live-stock business, of course, for the shorter the haul the less shrinkage in weight of cattle on the hoof. The roads which reached the East by roundabout routes got none.

The Grand Trunk, running through Canada, had practically no live-stock business. So its officials were delighted to get a share of the traffic in meat since they could not have it alive. They were glad to set a fair rate on dressed beef. They welcomed the resulting revenue. One other railroad used occasionally to accept a little of our dressed beef for the East, but only in small quantities at the low rate.

Father used to meet in New York the chairman of the Trunk Line Association, a German named Albert Fink. He and Fink would argue the dressed-meat rate by the hour and never get anywhere. Fink had his orders from the railroads and could not budge an inch.

Because father saw that the only way he could possibly get anywhere was by tact, he used tact for ten years, or as close an approach to tact as was possible under the circumstances. Meanwhile his beef for

points around New York City was turned over by
the Grand Trunk to American roads at Buffalo and
for New England points at other junctions nearer to
this market. The American roads charged local
rates on these hauls, which made them tremendously
expensive as freight went in those days.

He kept this up until the Interstate Commerce Act
was passed in 1887. Then the railroads had to take
his commodities at a fair rate and had to desist from
other practices which had stood in the way of freely
shipping meat to the East. It closed a long argument between father and Fink!

His serious difficulties in shipping beef had started
almost simultaneously with the first trouble on trunk
line rates. G. F. Swift had shipped some dressed
beef experimentally in box cars in the winter of
'75-'76. He had not been at it long before the rate
situation first blocked him, then turned him to the
Grand Trunk.

Technical difficulties of carrying dressed meat a
thousand miles in all weathers were, however, very
real. The first car of beef he shipped was an ordinary box car with a temporary framing built inside
to suspend the carcasses from. It was shipped in
cool weather and the meat arrived sweet and edible.

Then followed experiments, directed at first to
mastering the difficulties of winter shipping. A box
car of beef might start out in zero weather and the
meat be frozen stiff before it left the Chicago city
limits. In Indiana it might encounter a warm wave

and thaw out. Then it might freeze again and thaw again before arriving at Fall River or Clinton. After this it would be in a good deal worse condition than if it had gone all the way either frozen or chilled.

Cars were sent carrying small stoves with a man along to tend the stoves. Various wrappings and packings were tried. And finally the conclusion was plain that the beef lost in no way except appearance if it arrived frozen and was thawed out gradually.

This was in the winter before the butcher-gang came from Assonet to work in Billy Moore's slaughterhouse. The cattle that father sent dressed this winter were killed for him by G. H. Hammond for a slaughtering toll. When spring came in 1876 he gave up the experiment for a few months and went back to shipping cattle.

Hammond was, I think, the first man to ship beef commercially in refrigerator cars. He had at this time a handful of refrigerator cars which he used for shipping beef east. He was reasonably successful at it and had made a modest start toward attaining what father had in mind.

But G. F. Swift's energy and vision were destined to make a bigger thing of it than Hammond could make it. Hammond was using the idea as an auxiliary money-maker, something that yielded him a good steady little profit month in and month out. Father, once he had the device mastered, used it to build an industry such as had never been dreamed of before.

His first effort was to get the railroads to build

cars. The railroads as a class did not want dressed-beef traffic, much less were they going to encourage it. Finally it narrowed down to the Grand Trunk. But the Grand Trunk would not build the refrigerator cars, even if guaranteed a steady volume of traffic for them summer and winter. It was experimental.

Development of a satisfactory refrigerator car was being pushed from two sides at that time. On the one hand was the need to carry dressed beef from Middle West to East. But far more urgent was the demand for cars which would enable the farmers of the Pacific Coast to carry to eastern markets the fruits which they had in such abundance but could not sell. The coast had been growing in population and in fruit culture since the transcontinental railroads had been completed only a few years before. It was pressing hard for some means to market the perishable products of its fruit farms.

Outside the fruit belts of the United States, people seem to think of the refrigerator car as an appurtenance of the packing industry. Actually, by recent figures, there are several times as many refrigerator cars carrying fresh fruit, vegetables, and the like, as there are owned by packers and used principally for meat products. While G. F. Swift struggled to make progress to forward his ideas of shipping beef, a real effort was being made in many quarters to produce a satisfactory refrigerator car. Some had already been built which came pretty close to doing what they were supposed to.

Father rented such of these as he could get. In them he shipped beef east to his own wholesale market at Clinton, Massachusetts, and to Anthony, Swift & Company at Fall River. He even managed to get a couple of distributors and to keep them supplied with Chicago-dressed beef. The first two customers to push his product in the East—outside of the two firms which he owned or had an interest in—were Francis Jewett, of Lowell, and I. M. Lincoln, of Providence.

When the railroads refused to build refrigerator cars for him to ship in, he approached the Michigan Car Company, of Detroit. The McMillen family owned this concern. They were rich and had a leaning toward an undertaking which might make them a profitable future market if they took a little chance in the present.

Reduced to its barest terms, G. F. Swift's proposal to the owners was that they build him some refrigerator cars and let him pay for them out of their earnings. They took a chance with him, even though they did not know that the cars would earn. To be sure, they retained a hold on them—something on the order of a mortgage which was, I think, the forerunner of the modern equipment trust. But the cars would be worth little to anyone unless they could yield a profit. And if G. F. Swift could not make them pay, then the Michigan Car Company stood a slender chance of ever being paid for them.

He paid fifteen per cent down, as I recall the

transaction, with the remainder to be paid monthly out of earnings. It was a remarkable deal for those days. Car builders were used to getting cash for their products. The railroads had not yet been reduced to the intricate ways of financing which have become general as operating costs have risen.

Patents had offered a real obstacle, too. The patent situation on refrigerator cars was a maze. Hammond had certain patents which made his refrigerator cars satisfactory. There was a Tiffany patent, a Zimmerman patent. There was the Anderson car, the Wickes car. Not one of them was absolutely right for the purpose; all of them had some good features.

So father made what arrangements he could with the patentees and designed a car which seemed to incorporate the best features of them all. This was the design by which his first ten cars were being built in Detroit. Once he could have the cars rolling, he felt sure he would begin making money fast. The cars were completed and success seemed just around the corner.

But before they could be moved and put to work, Hammond brought injunction proceedings. He claimed an infringement and he tied up in the builder's yards all ten of those urgently needed cars.

Here they remained for several months. Legal procedure is always too slow to help much in a situation of this sort. No matter how father might fight it in the courts, at best it would take months or years before he could hope to have his cars released for his use.

Once more he resorted to tact. It was a blue time for him. But he managed to convince another wealthy man of the possibilities in those cars. This man lent him the money to put up as a bond with the court to guarantee Hammond against any damages the cars might do him. By hustling around, father soon had the ten cars hauling beef east for him. Eventually his claims were upheld. The courts ruled, "No infringement."

But even after it was working, almost nobody had much confidence in his plan of slaughtering cattle in Chicago and selling the meat in the East. "Stave's Wild West scheme" it came to be known among the Cape Cod relatives.

Within two years the Yankee had over a hundred cars running from the Yards to the East. They were all making money. Still no one took him seriously. Others before him had tried shipping beef east and had failed. Everyone prophesied that it would break him. He kept on, getting a tremendous head start while the others waited for him to fail. By 1880 the refrigerator car, and with it G. F. Swift's method of dressing beef in Chicago, was indisputably a success.

Once he got the refrigerator cars running, his difficulties were still on the increase. His technical troubles with the cars and with getting the meat chilled properly before hanging it in the cars very nearly broke him. Ruin was so close several times, in fact, that good active hustling was all that saved him.

Aside from these troubles, he had to develop all kinds of auxiliary equipment for his refrigerator cars and his beef coolers. He had to buy ice-harvesting rights in lakes all over northern Illinois and southern Wisconsin so that he might have the ice for cooling his beef and loading the ice boxes of his cars at Chicago. He had to develop icing stations all the way across the country to his markets in the East—the railroads would not build them. Then he had to get the ice-harvesting facilities to supply these stations. He had to build ice houses of huge capacity. His ice-consuming capacity was by the wave of a hand and the development of an idea greater than any other ice user's in the country.

These stations have, for the most part, long since gone out of our hands. The Interstate Commerce Commission ruled on complaint of other packers that we could no longer hold icing stations, since our icing stations gave us a small profit on all competitors' shipments. So the stations were sold to the railroads, which by then were glad to take them over. And refrigeration by mechanical means had displaced ice to such an extent that only a small percentage of all of our refrigeration requirements were supplied by natural ice.

But the means by which father built them, financed them, and maintained them—all of this is with us as vitally as it was then. For it comprised the principal

essentials of building a business under great handicaps of inadequate capital. He built under those
circumstances. What is more, he built both fast and
sound.

CHAPTER XI

NEVER STAY BEATEN

NEVER admit it even when somebody's beat you."

My father draped his angular person over my old-fashioned roll-top desk and gratuitously offered me this bit of friendly advice a hundred times, I suppose, during the '80s and '90s. To be sure, he vented a Jovian wrath more times than that when he had me beaten on some point and I would not admit it. But he seldom intended his generalizations of conduct to apply to his managers and his sons in their relations with him!

Had he been more the philosopher and less the man of action, father would have stated his advice a little differently. As he exemplified his maxim in daily life, in his idiom it should have been: "Never admit it even to yourself when somebody's beat you." He never admitted it, even to himself.

"Let's talk about something else," he would direct on those rare occasions when a manager or one of the boys cornered him and penned him in with heaped-up facts. Translated, this meant, "Go ahead, do it your way. But *I* won't admit you have me beaten!"

He was never small about it. He did not reserve this attitude for his subordinates or for the moments

193

when, perhaps, a superintendent proved conclusively
that his pet way of splitting a hog was far ahead of
the plan his chief was sponsoring. What was true in
the *minutiae* of his daily work was quite as noticeable in his moments of great crisis.

He would never admit a defeat, even to himself.
He never knew when he was licked. If he had recognized a number of different occasions when he was
genuinely worsted, his history must inevitably have
been different.

Several times his business was in such shape that I
cannot yet quite understand how he managed to pull
it through. Certainly he would have lost it if ever
he had recognized its hopeless state. In the early
years at Chicago he was frequently so deeply involved
that one marvels he came through at all.

A man who was associated with Gustavus Franklin
Swift for many years, at first back in Brighton and
later in Chicago, always declared that his friend and
employer progressed as he did through two closely
related reasons: "He had abiding faith in his ultimate success. He was afraid of nothing."

These are the only explanations I can offer for several extraordinary phenomena which acquaintance-
ship with his career brings to mind. How was he
able to take hold of the refrigerator car—something
which others had tried, which some in fact had used
—and make it in his hands a tool a thousand times
more potent than ever it had seemed? How did he
manage, in a field where others were large and pow-

erful, to grow from insignificance at a speed which even in this day of larger affairs seems dizzy, to overcome obstacles which from this perspective seem to have been insurmountable, and to become eventually the leader in his new industry?

His faith, his lack of fear, these made possible what he accomplished. He simply could not dignify discouraging circumstances by letting them discourage him. He went his way serenely ignoring what by all calculations should have disheartened him.

Had he recognized facts which were as plain as the nose on his face he would have quit and lost his business in '93. He would never have got past the discouraging times of the late '70s when daily he staked more than he could afford to lose. He staked it on the performance of faulty refrigerator cars which perversely failed to keep their perishable contents cold. He staked it on imperfect beef coolers which took the most inopportune occasions to obstinately refuse to chill the natural heat out of the fresh-killed carcasses in time for them to be shipped.

He was playing for big stakes, playing long shots to win. The odds against him were his faulty coolers and faulty cars. When he won, when a shipment got through in good shape, he made a good profit. When he lost, when a car of beef arrived good only for dumping into the bay at Fall River, then the loss should have staggered him.

But it did not. Such a loss failed to disturb him. "It will be all right," he would assure the rest of us as we discussed our bad luck in the depths of our discouragement. Then with all good cheer he would promptly entrust another half-dozen loads of the precious beef to his fallible cars. Probably this would get through in good shape and so would the next shipment. Then, just as he was getting in the clear with his profits on successful shipments, something would go wrong again.

It took only two or three cars of soured beef to wipe out his gains on a good many cars that arrived sweet and salable. Two successive losses of good size frequently put him in the red for an amount beyond the limits of any other man's credit. Somehow, though, he would keep his courage up, refuse to admit he was in a corner, get more money if the case was that desperate.

"The trouble is, we don't quite know how to do it right," he would admit with not a trace of discouragement. "We'll get it, though. We'll learn." Then he would set about experimenting some more, watching even more carefully than before to make sure that he overlooked no known precaution.

Many a hot July and August night he got on a horse and rode over to the packing house at midnight or later. He would go straight to the coolers and eye the thermometers. Then he would be after the foreman. "You've got to get those men to shoveling more ice and more salt," he would direct. "Let's see the temperature come down five degrees." And though it meant vigil to the moment of going to his

THE ORIGINAL WINDLASS USED BY G. F. SWIFT
FOR HOISTING STEER AFTER KILLING--
BARNSTABLE, 1861-1869.

THE ORIGINAL BULL-RING USED
BY G. F. SWIFT FOR PULLING
ANIMAL DOWN FOR SLAUGHTER.

desk for the morning mail, father would walk among the men urging them to greater efforts until the tell-tale mercury column dropped to a reassuring depth.

Inventors busied themselves those days with coolers and refrigerator cars. Orchardmen beyond the Sierras clamored for something on wheels that would roll into Hoboken yards with its fragile freight all toothsome. Swift, the Yankee of the Yards, chafed for the chance to try any device which might serve surely to haul his Chicago beef sweet and edible to New England and New York. The world's mechanically minded worked to perfect the means.

But they seemed to crawl. Progress must be faster if this pioneer was to build an industry and control the large share of it his heart was set on. So besides having a look at any device brought to him, he likewise experimented on improvements to find what he must have.

Before he came to Chicago, he had at Fall River installed a refrigerator built by the Chase patent—then rebuilt it to make it work. At Chicago he built Chase refrigerators and Zimmerman refrigerators—and rebuilt them. He and his superintendent worked continually at improving these carcass chillers. They would build a model incorporating some hopeful idea for circulating air through every part of the compartment, the basic problem of refrigeration. Then they would send smoke through the chambers, so that their eyes might trace the currents.

Painfully, step by step they worked out the fundamental laws of refrigeration which are generally known today. They were not scientists looking for principles. They were practical packing-house men in search of ways to chill beef carcasses properly. Today we know that they discovered the principles and might well have written monographs and textbooks on refrigeration had they been so inclined.

All the while they were working with cars, too. Father tried out first, as I recall it, the Wickes car and the Anderson car. Anderson relied on the natural circulation of air through the ice chambers and the beef chamber—but the car was so built that this circulation took place only imperfectly. Wickes employed in his cars a contraption which hitched a fan to the car axle, thus blowing the cold air through the car.

It was an excellent device, barring a few flaws. When the car stopped moving, if it went on a siding or if the locomotive broke down or if a wreck stopped the train, then circulation stopped with it and consequently so did the refrigeration. Likewise if the belt broke or loosened. We lost a good deal of meat first and last in Wickes cars which were delayed. If the train kept moving, then the meat arrived in perfect condition—always assuming that the fan kept blowing!

Because the laws of refrigeration were not understood, we had difficulty in chilling carcass meats in quantity at the packing house. When we killed perhaps thirty or forty cattle a day, chilling was easy.

But as the day's slaughter mounted into the hundreds, the carcasses contained in the aggregate a great deal of heat when they came into the cold rooms. It was like bringing in so many loads of hot bricks. They raised the temperature effectively and frequently held it high through the night until the next day's fresh kill came in to reinforce them. If this kept up for two or three days, perhaps every carcass in the cooler was still warm to the touch.

When this happened and the warm meats went into the cars, they might be chilled in transit. But if a car happened to be one of the faulty ones, then its load was likely to sour long before it got to market.

In the late summer of '77 father got hold of the Zimmerman car, a great improvement over the others. But when he tried the same principle in a carcass chiller, it failed utterly.

Not until the summer of '79 did he get the proper design for his beef coolers. He had nothing but grief until then, when he got in an improved Chase patent refrigerator and added to it his own refinements for air circulation. Once this was working, he built on the same design several chillers of about one hundred-carcass capacity each. He insisted that beef must hang here between two and three days as a minimum.

Thus his Zimmerman car and his Chase cooler put him in what was by contrast with his previous experience extremely good shape. They left him free to work on other major problems. It was sev-

eral years later that he discovered the Chase principle produced a better car, too.

But even when he had the Chase cooler and the
Zimmerman car, the worst of his early troubles were
over. He made money very fast. He could undersell
the local slaughterers of the East and still make more
profit per dollar of sales. He enjoyed a fixed differ-
ential in his favor, the saving he made by paying
freight on only the edible portions of the beef animal.

The technical difficulty of getting chillers and cars
to do what they were supposed to was only part of
his troubles as a pioneer. Beef spoiled in transit or
in the underchilled coolers. It cost him lots of money,
too, when lots of money was exactly what he lacked—
still this was only a beginning to his woes.

G. F. Swift's total wealth at the time he settled
his partnership with J. A. Hathaway was around
thirty thousand dollars. He had made little during
the early years, for what he made on successful shipments he lost on the failures. And he poured good
money after bad on experiments with coolers and
cars—experiments which advanced his knowledge of
refrigeration and so in the long run amply repaid
their cost. But at the time they looked like dead loss.
Dead loss was the one thing he could not afford.

Meanwhile he was having to put money and still
more money in auxiliary equipment to further his
refrigeration. Mechanical refrigeration was not in
use then—at least not in packing houses. Our first
mechanical refrigeration unit was built in our first

pork-packing plant in 1887. It was our maiden step
from our bondage to natural ice.

He had become by his adoption of the principle of
slaughtering in one place and selling the meat a thousand miles away the country's largest user of ice. To
supply ice in the quantities he needed and at the
places he needed it, he provided the extensive facilities already mentioned.

Financing all this extension was a real burden. It
came when money was most urgently needed in other
divisions of the business—and before investors were
eager to put in their money.

When father needed money in these days he usually went out and hustled for it. His presence
inspired confidence. People usually believed in him
from the first meeting. So, with his wide acquaintance in New England's beef and live-stock trades, he
managed selling shares or borrowing money rather
easily.

When everything else failed, he would go to D.
M. Anthony and to John Sawyer in Boston. He
always managed to get money from them. A good
many times during those blue times of '77 and '78
their funds, wheedled from them by his persuasive
enthusiasm, were all that saved him. But if he had
ever let himself see there was doubt of his pulling
through, he must many times have given in to the
overwhelming odds.

His capital was habitually depleted. Frozen assets
of one sort and another were almost the rule at first.

And while in a brisk market his business could have been sold on the auction block to yield enough for the creditors and leave a little something over for the owners, still he met the technical definition of insolvency. He could not have met his obligations at the time they fell due.

Somehow, though, he would fight through the troubles. He would not admit, even to himself, that he was beaten. So he was not beaten. He would go to a creditor for an extension, or to a banker with another note to replace the one which would soon fall due—and he would get what he went after.

These were growing pains, these financial troubles. The last of them and the most serious were the troubles of '93. He had got through one crisis after another by increasing the company's stock. The assets had grown considerably faster than the capital; book value was always considerably above par value. So he got more money into the business by issuing more stock when he needed it.

The business was coming to the place where it would need a lot more money to take care of its rapid expansion. Father saw this in '92. He also suspected the approach of the financial panic which appeared by May of '93. He did not, however, expect it so soon.

An unusually large cash dividend was declared at the end of 1892—something like twenty-four per cent, as I recall it. And, on the heels of this, the stockholders authorized a large increase of the capital stock. This issue was offered to the stockholders very soon after.

But it did not sell well at all. There had, of course, been in the directors' minds the idea that the big dividend would make the stock sell out in a hurry. But the stockholders were already feeling the pinch of the money tightness which was to clamp them three months later in the great panic. Thankfully they accepted the cash dividend and thankfully they used it to help themselves out of their other financial difficulties! As to the new stock issue, it would be a nice thing to buy, they figured. But when you haven't the money, you can't buy. So they didn't buy.

This is really why the panic of '93 hit Swift & Company hard. The treasury was bare of ready cash—and the proceeds of the stock issue which had been expected to yield plenty to carry through the slump failed to materialize. It was perhaps six months before the stock issue sold clean. By then the business was out of the woods. Father, aided by L. A. Carton, had managed to finance the business on its own assets. For half a year the business had been living, like the traditional desert camel, on its hump.

Details of that fight have been told in a preceding chapter. It was a magnificent struggle, the more remarkable that it was successful. If the head of the business had been willing to face the situation with a real recognition of how desperate it was, I do not believe he could have pulled it through. He would not admit even to himself that he was beaten. He laughed at the facts, though he relaxed meanwhile not an ounce of his effort to overcome them.

His attitude toward the whole affair came up one day in a conversation with his head butcher. The butcher was getting fifteen dollars a week—he wanted a raise. That a panic was raging meant nothing to him. The demand might have exasperated anyone at such a time. Strangely enough it did not annoy his chief.

"I'll tell you what I'll do," the boss countered to the astounded packing-house man. "I'll trade you my profits this week for your wages." On that jocular basis, the employee soon found himself goodnaturedly agreeing that he didn't want a raise!

With the autumn of '93, Swift & Company was done with growing pains. Then it was that the business reached maturity. Within a year or two the continual shortage of ready money was over. Now its head could take his ease, with the business grown to a size greater than any other industrial concern in the country and with money plentiful.

It was the first time. From the very start, when he came to the Chicago Yards as a Yankee cattle buyer, G. F. Swift had been cramped for cash. When he started out in the dressed-beef business, then he was indeed of small financial importance beside Armour and Morris.

Armour & Company in 1875 handled no beef, no mutton. They were pork packers only. In cool weather they slaughtered, pickled, cured, and smoked pork products. These they shipped all over the world. When warm weather came once more they shut down their packing houses.

This, by the way, was true packing. The modern packer devotes only a part of his effort to packing. Packing involves preserving meats so that they will not spoil, at least not spoil easily. Hams, bacon, corned beef, smoked tongue, smoked sausage, salt pork, these are packed products. The dressed meat business is in no sense packing, though the word has come to include a great many nonpacking activities. G. F. Swift was in the dressed-meat business from 1876, but except in a very incidental way he was not a packer until 1887.

Morris & Company did no packing in 1875. It dealt only in fresh beef, as locally around Chicago as did Anthony, Swift & Company around Fall River. For beef could not be shipped dressed, a minor quantity always excepted which was salted and pickled principally for export.

P. D. Armour and Nelson Morris were rich men and older men than G. F. Swift. By the time they realized he was not going to fail, he had such a head start that they never overtook him.

From the time he had his refrigerator car lines going, he was the largest slaughterer of beef. He soon added mutton and was almost immediately at the top on this score. When pork was added, in 1887, he began dealing in huge quantities of fresh dressed pork—though it was a good many years before the pork products business, the hams and bacons, and the like, overtook that of his established competitors.

But even when the business was going well, he had his periodical troubles. One of these was the oleo oil patent suit. Father thought he had the rights to make oleo oil. A patent-holder thought that he had not. So the patent-holder brought suit for infringement.

The head of our company was put in the situation where he had to get that whole set of patents adjudged open to the world, else his business would have been liable for so much money that it could not have survived. This patent suit made little impression outside the packing industry. But every packer knew it was a fight to the death. By the time the decisions had been appealed and reappealed and a final unreversible decision handed down, anyone was at liberty to make oleo oil by any process he cared to use. Once more his refusal to admit he was beaten had won the day. For at the outset, if ever a lawsuit looked hopeless this one did.

Another set of troubles—minor perhaps but none the less obstinate—were those with the British distributors already referred to. They were willing to handle American beef. But because it was not native to the British Isles, their sound British instincts told them it must be inferior.

So they cut the meat differently from the standard way. This made it look inferior. Actually it was up to the standard of the best British beef ever produced anywhere. Ours was fine, clean meat. It did not take a cynic to have his reasonable doubts about the cleanliness of a good deal of the British beef.

Father was forever turning up at Smithfield market in the gray London dawn with his cheery insistence on having his beef cut properly. Although British conservatism seemed a hopeless obstacle, in time he wore it down—for he could not see the obstacle as hopeless.

He went at it cheerfully, won his point as he always did, and soon his beef was in demand as the finest obtainable. Before long he had to open branch houses all over Great Britain and Ireland to accommodate the trade.

He encountered a comparable task when he went at the job of feeding Chicago-dressed beef to the hidebound, rockbound conservatives of New England and New York. Eat meat dressed a thousand miles away? No Yankee had ever been served a steak which originated more than a few miles from the stove that cooked it, no sir, not if he knew it! To people accustomed to having a slaughterhouse just outside the limits of every town, the very idea of Chicago-dressed beef was repugnant. The meat was actually fresher in condition if not in time. It had been produced in cleanliness instead of in a filthy small-town shambles. The cattle were in better condition when slaughtered. But all this made little difference. Prejudice is founded on feelings, not on knowledge. When one puts his mind to work on a question, then prejudice cannot remain.

Father would not admit that a prejudice could stop him. He wore down that Yankee prejudice—mind you, he was doing this in the self-same weeks when he was watching his smoke currents eddy through embryonic chillers and refrigerator cars, on the day before or the day after he was buying an ice house with fifty thousand dollars which he confidently expected to get from selling stock to a friend. He was doing it between appointments at Brighton and Boston where he would somehow borrow the money to make up his losses on spoiled shipments. How any man could carry so many activities and perform them all so well has never been answered to my satisfaction. Yet I was with him several hours a day while he kept the equivalent of a fish-bowl, a cannon ball, and a live rabbit in mid air. It was uncanny.

His wide acquaintance in the live-stock and meat trade of the East served him in getting distribution, just as it served him in getting money. In fact, the two often went hand in hand. He would sign up a wholesale dealer to carry our dressed beef; then before he got through he would sell that dealer a small block of Swift stock. He got not only an outlet, but along with it the sincere loyalty of a partner. And he got the money he was needing so badly all the while. In the course of a few years he and his brother Edwin worked out several hundreds of these

partnership arrangements, usually with a Swift interest in the distributing business as a double bond.

After the panic of 1893 had passed and money was
easy in the business, an idea began to develop tending
toward consolidation. The steel consolidations had
just been completed. Consolidation was in the air.

So father, J. O. Armour, and Edward Morris
formed the National Packing Company in 1902. It
was capitalized at fifteen million dollars. Its com-
ponents were a group of "small packers," the term
which includes all but the handful of very large
companies. The plan was to continue with the
merger, taking in the smaller of the large packers.
Then, when all of these were welded into one unit,
the National Packing Company would absorb the
"Big Three," Swift, Armour, and Morris. It was
an ambitious plan.

But public opinion was too strong against it. Perhaps if father had lived, it might have gone through
—though I doubt it. He died early in 1903. As
public opinion rose against the enterprise, the terms
on which the bankers would finance the merger rose
at the same pace. Once the financing charges had
begun their climb, the plan died of its own weight.
Eventually by court order the National Packing
Company was dissolved, and the smaller companies
which composed it were returned to their previous
owners.

So father's last great business dream fell through
when he was no longer here to know it.

Of all the major plans he had ever made, this alone he failed to push through to successful, profitable completion.

Can there be a more forceful, compact way of summing up G. F. Swift's record?

INDEX

INDEX

213